DIARY OF A

Real Estate

Rookie

My Year of Flipping, Selling, and Rebuilding— and What I Learned

(The Hard Way)

ALISON ROGERS

This publication is designed to provide accurate and authoritative information in regard to the subject matter covered. It is sold with the understanding that the publisher is not engaged in rendering legal, accounting, or other professional service. If legal advice or other expert assistance is required, the services of a competent professional should be sought.

Vice President and Publisher: Maureen McMahon
Editorial Director: Jennifer Farthing
Acquisitions Editor: Michael Sprague
Development Editor: Joshua Martino
Production Editor: Karina Cueto
Production Artist: PBS and Associates
Production Designer: Ivelisse Robles Marrero
Cover Designer: Rattray Design

Published by Kaplan Publishing, a division of Kaplan, Inc.
1 Liberty Plaza, 24th Floor
New York, NY 10006

Portions of this book appeared as a column on Inman News.
Inman News is the leading source for independent news, analysis, research,
and events about real estate. For more information, visit *www.inman.com.*

Printed in the United States of America

June 2007
07 08 09 10 9 8 7 6 5 4 3 2 1

ISBN-13: 978-1-4277-5465-3

Kaplan Publishing books are available at special quantity discounts to use for sales promotions, employee premiums, or educational purposes. Please email our Special Sales Department to order or for more information at kaplanpublishing@kaplan.com, or write to Kaplan Publishing, 1 Liberty Plaza, 24th Floor, New York, NY 10006.

Contents

Part II: *New York*

Part III: *More Tips From the Front Porch*

Introduction

(An Idea of What You're Getting Into)

MORE THAN SIX million Americans move each year. If anecdotal evidence is anything to go by, 5.9 million of them hate their real estate agents.

So how did I end up going into a profession that ranks below "vampire" on the trust scale? And why should that interest you? The answer to the first question is: I had a midlife crisis. I had been a real estate journalist at a big newspaper—the *New York Post*—and I got married. It seemed important, if I was ever going to have a more interesting career and up my income, to try out those things before the kids came.

The answer to the second question is: Things didn't turn out like I planned. I ended up exploring a much wider area of real estate than I thought, from flipping to landlording to brokerage, and at every turn stuff kept happening to me that wasn't in the books. So I wrote my own.

Diary of a Real Estate Rookie is actually two books: a memoir of my first year in real estate—which was also my first year of marriage—and a personal finance guide to buying, selling, and renting. The year—as you'll see from the following memoir—was quite an adventure. I initially quit my job to partner with an established New Jersey real estate firm as a "flipper." My partners, whom I call the Power Trio, would provide the capital and the expertise. The deal was that I would provide the sweat, in exchange for one-third of the profits.

Well, that didn't work. When I started the venture, I didn't think I was a naïve idiot; I had bought and sold real estate for a six-figure profit. I had owned a co-op, a condo, and a house; I had been a landlady for four years. I had renovated a bathroom, and owned two properties at once, and I generally thought I knew what I was doing. Yet I started to go broke, *because of real estate agents.* I'd like to think it was not treachery but thoughtlessness on their part, yet the impact was no less harmful for all that.

So I turned tail back to New York—where I've lived for nearly two decades—to get my real estate license. And two parallel careers started to grow. The first was that I started to become an unusual kind of real estate agent—I was determined to be different, because I had empathy. I had had smoke blown in my face, and I had suffered mightily as a result. I didn't want to do that to other people; customers, not surprisingly, started to respond to that. I decided moreover that if I could just give my average Village or Tribeca client the level of service they normally got from their Mercedes dealer, I would be way ahead of the game, and I was. It's sad to think about: There are 1.3 million Realtors in the United States, and all I had to do to beat the average was to aspire to be a decent car salesman.

My second unplanned career avenue was that I turned into a kind of industry commentator. I had been writing weekly about my adventures for Inman News, which is a real estate industry news site, and as "Diary of a Flipper" (New Jersey) turned into "Diary of a Rookie" (New York), I seemed to snag more and more readers. When I was pitching a listing in a brownstone off Central Park and someone turned to me in the hallway and said, "Hey, you're Rookie," I realized I had something.

The more I told it "like it is," the more I got requests to tell it. Now, you have to understand that Manhattan has been one of the fizziest real estate markets on the planet: I have seen sell-out sales parties with water dripping through the ceiling of the display apartment. I have been in a penthouse where the Corcoran broker, offering the apartment for $3.99 million, had not managed to take away the show sheets left by the Stribling broker, who had offered the unit just a few months earlier at $2.77 million. Just yesterday, I was in a model unit priced at $2.3 million, where, I swear to heaven, I could have done a better job installing the floors with a staple gun. The sales agent told me with cool effrontery that they would do a better job in the real units. And such is the mania of the market that I walked out thinking, *I wonder if my client can afford to pass this up?*

So that's what the book's "Front Porch" material is: an attempt to provide personal finance and home advice, of a fairly basic kind, in the middle of madness. Unlike a go-go stock cycle, real estate is a mania where it's hard to sit on the sidelines—we don't all have to own WorldCom, but we do all have to live somewhere. Yet a lot of the homes that are available now are overpriced trash; I've been inside them, and I know. So while I can't lower the prices, I tried to make my tips as timeless as possible. If you need more, visit my Web site at *www.frontporchllc.com*.

What else? Well, some of this tale was written down as it happened, as a weekly column for Inman.com, and some of it is memoir that got written down (or as my dearest husband would say, "reinterpreted") later. But everything in this book, including the heroin incident and the underwear incident, really happened, and happened to me. My darling friend Persephone even allowed me to use her name, in addition to taking the leap to be my very first client.

Also, I see things through a filter of upbringing (grew up in Little Rock, Arkansas), race (white and grew up in Little Rock, where schooling and sometimes housing were fought over with guns), and class (upper-middle, Harvard-educated bourgeois bohemian). I tried not to shy away from these perceptions even if they reflected somewhat poorly upon me. Despite the best efforts of my copy editor, I use the words *Realtor, broker,* and *real estate agent,* all of which have specific shades of meaning, somewhat interchangeably; ditto *customer* and *client.* I am not trying to be careless here, but the people we are working for, I find, do not worry so much about the language and our industry's need to split hairs about it; they want us to do better.

Prologue

Leaving Rockefeller Center

*(In Which the Author Explains Her Midlife Crisis and Her
Confidence That She Can Found a Business with $16,000)*

BY 2003, I was 36 years old and I had been humming the Mary Tyler
Moore theme for 15 years. That's how long I had been living and working in New York, living in cramped and buggy apartments, thinking that
maybe, just maybe, something magical was going to happen to me. As a
Phi Beta Kappa, *summa cum laude* graduate of Harvard, I was fast and smart
and funny and hardworking—but I was also, as my old boss Roz Berlin
once said, a *hitzkop*—a hothead. I fell in love with every new idea I had,
and let them tug me around like a weathervane.

By this point, I was a mid-level reporter, writer, and editor. I had
been drawn to journalism because I thought it would be fast-paced, stimu-
lating, and ever-changing; in reality, it was fast-paced, laborious, and repetitious. Did I say repetitious? It was.

In a last, desperate bid to make something of myself, I threw all my
weight at my then-current employer, the Wall Street newspaper *The Daily
Deal*. I had been in the same job, doing the same thing, for ever-so-aching-
ly long (in real terms, a year and a half, but I felt so far behind). I started to
push and shove for an overseas posting, which, though not a promotion,

would look like résumé movement and at least be an adventure. Everyone I knew seemed to think this would be a good move, except for one tall, dark, and nerdy guy I'd met just six months before. We'd had such fun, he and I, going to movies and hanging out in the park and volunteering at the homeless shelter. How could we do those things if I were in London and he were still in New York?

So when my friend Stephie Jo told me the *New York Post* was looking for a real estate editor to create a new section, I jumped at the chance to do something new and stay in New York. A chance to have a hit.

The *New York Post* offices are every romantic's idea of a newsroom: reporters swarming around cramped desks with curled-up old newspapers and boxes of junk piled everywhere. The Sixth Avenue headquarters is so inky, jam-packed, and buggy it would make Jann Wenner go into cardiac arrest; tell that to any *Post* old-timer and they'll reminisce about the paper's former offices at the South Street Seaport, where mice literally dropped from the ceiling.

I interviewed there with Faye Penn, the features editor. When I met Faye she looked like a comic-strip character: a grown woman with golden Shirley Temple locks, fierce cat's-eye glasses, and an eight-months-pregnant belly. She ran features at the *Post,* a newspaper that seemed to have little contact with the outside media world, so I knew almost nothing about her. I was so hungry for the job I had put together a mock-up of the new section; I practically offered to deliver her baby. I begged: I was bored, I needed a challenge, and I loved the tabloid punch of the *Post.* Yes, I would work 24 hours a day to create the greatest real estate section ever. Yes, I had personal experience in real estate: seven closings in six years. Working on a journalist's salary, I owned a place in the city and an investment house at the beach. I had lived in a brownstone, lived in a ghetto, and played landlady. And what about London—would I screw over everyone at my old job who had fought so hard to give me such a great opportunity? Of course I would.

There was just the little matter of salary: I was making $99K per year at *The Daily Deal,* and had just used that as a basis to buy a condo in Manhattan after being absent from the city for two years. Because I already had an investment house at the beach, my housing costs were nearly $55K, defrayed by a rental income of $15K. Spending 40 percent of my gross income on housing may have been unwise, but it was a bull market and real estate seemed like the right place to be. The trouble was the *Post* was notoriously cheap, and the budget for the leader of the unlaunched real estate section was frugal—how could they pay well until they'd seen a success? Faye asked me if I really thought I could stand to take a salary cut to $80K. *Take it, take it!* the little *hitzkop* voice said. *You need a hit.*

I asked for a six-month review to accelerate my raise schedule. "It would be tough but I love real estate, and I'm dying to be at the *Post,*" I said.

Faye offered me the job and shook my hand. "We'll make it up to you."

Two years later, I had barely fought my way back to $90K, and my pissed-off-ness knew no bounds. I had had my hit: The paper gained 30,000 readers (off a base in the high 400,000s) in the first six weeks after we launched. Media recognition? The mighty *New York Times* had copied our formula for its real estate section relaunch. Financial success? Between revenue and circulation increases, I figured my section brought the money-losing *Post* around $5 million over the two years I was there.

While I had gotten a $5,000 raise at my six-month mark, after that I found nothing but battlefield: We didn't have enough advertisers, would I please stop pandering to advertisers; we didn't have enough readers, would I please stop doing TV interviews to gain readers; we didn't have interesting national content, would I please stop wasting my time talking to this Bob Vila person (the Aussies, of course, did not know who he was) because even though he offered to do columns for $400 a pop, I was just tying up the lawyers arguing over his contracts and not really doing *my* job, whatever that was.

As I became progressively more embittered, I took to sporting lots of *Post* giveaway paraphernalia to work—shirts, baseball caps, umbrellas—and began to mutter to myself in the hallways—a line that usually came out as, *I made Rupert Murdoch five million bucks and all I got was five thousand dollars and a hat.*

The final straw came over a conference-linked special section. The business-side guys had made a deal for the sponsorship of the Harlem Home Fair, a position the racist *Post* sorely needed. In doing so, they'd given away the section's cover, promising to do a bunch of stories about Harlem. Journalistically, you're not supposed to let your advertisers or sponsors know what you're writing about, let alone negotiate with them. Of course this rule is broken all the time, and this breach happened in meetings at which the editor was present. Or so I was told; of course *I* wasn't important enough to be at them.

When Harlem Week rolled around, I had only prepared one cover package: Harlem, the one we'd sold. Col Allan, the editor who had supposedly signed on to this gross breach of journalistic ethics, decided that I had perpetrated it. He yelled at me for three straight days. I had spent two years on Wall Street, where every mistake I made lost someone a million dollars, and I was used to getting cussed at, but this was three days of red-faced hollering, coming out of the mouth of a man that grown men fear. At one point I walked out of Col's office and nearly fainted at the Metro Editor's feet.

Understand that being yelled at by an Australian is a kind of like being yelled at by a Texan: you realize that while you can hang in the fight, you ain't gonna win. Since at heart I'm a Southern girl, I at least found my grit and hung in. Maybe we had come to the Harlem cover story for the wrong reasons, but we had an independently reported package that was quite good, and how could it be wrong, in 2005, to tell our readers about one of the hottest home markets in the world? (Thinking, *Gee, where were this newspaper's ethics when it declared the wrong guy as a vice-presidential candidate? When Page Six wrote up that someone had lunch with an executive, a grave error because the guy turned out to be dead? And hey, where's the rest of the money you promised me?*)

I broke my poor crew's back to work up an entirely independent cover package—something extolling the virtues of suburban Connecticut, I think it was—and Col preferred Harlem to it, so the original package was published, just as I had asked. I had technically won, but we were done, Col and I, and the paper and I as well. The tabloid fun was over. I got married (the tall, dark, and nerdy guy had shown quite a bit of staying power) and spent two weeks on my honeymoon touring Peru. Faye left her job when I was in the rainforest, and a month after I came back, I quit.

So, out of disgust and motivated by greed, I went into real estate. There's a joke in the industry that real estate is no one's first career; it's always something people come to by default, seeking money. (Apparently, quite a lot of people, as there are more than a million registered Realtors in the United States.) I wanted what so many people want: a better income, a better life, room to raise my family near great schools, a job where I didn't get ass-draggy just thinking about starting my day. I felt I had little to show for my 18 years of corporate work; if I had been a cop, at least I would be nearing retirement by now.

I had a toehold in real estate, though, that many of my peers didn't have. I had found a New Jersey real estate firm that would help me flip houses—and they'd provide the capital. I was ready, I thought, to quit being a desk monkey and make the big money. Sure, there would be bobbles along the way, but this would be an adventure. I had convinced my darling handsome Ivan to marry me; clearly I was blessed and had a charmed life, and I could do anything. Why not take the risk now?

I took out a home equity line on the beach house, which gave me $26,000 (of which Citibank, the holder of my credit cards, promptly paid itself back $10,000 I owed them) and I got my Jersey partners to sign on to a business plan. I inked a deal with Web mogul Brad Inman to write a column about my rookie adventures in real estate; I figured that would cover one mortgage. Plus, surely there would be PR work; there had always been before.

For a hair-trigger *hitzkop,* I had thought long and hard about my escape from corporate America, and I was determined not to fail. *How could I fail?* I had connections: By the time I left, I knew by name the head of every single large brokerage in New York, and many in the tri-state area. Some had even sent me wedding presents from my registry. I had karma: I had seen Dolly Lenz (Barbra Streisand's broker) in a bar, and received her personal blessing. And I had glamour: To celebrate, my friend Barbara Wagner took me out to Nobu 57, one of New York's chicest restaurants. I remember that night so well; I was embarking on a great adventure, commemorated by mega-chef Drew Nieporent serving me a chipotle dish with his own hands.

This book is the story of the year after that. It is the story of my first year of business, and of my first year of marriage. It is a story of failure, and tears, and immense love. Don't worry, there are some pretty tricked-out luxury condos along the way.

Part I

New Jersey

Chapter 1

Back to School

(A Harvard Grad Gets the Beginnings of a Real Estate Education)

I HAD FORGOTTEN about linoleum.

I don't mean the stuff you might have in your kitchen; that's underfoot, you clean it every now and then (less often if you're me), and probably don't think about it. But remember good ol' classroom linoleum? That's the kind where you count the squares and scrutinize the edges to make sure they're lined up straight, and squint at the pattern of everyone's black heel marks to find the face of Jesus or the Fonz.

Suddenly I have 75 hours to get reacquainted. I decided to start making my fortune in New Jersey, and the route's first toll is the 75 hours of class time required of every real estate wannabe. (Potential flippers, I was told, ought to get licensed as real estate agents.) I had a full head of steam after quitting my job, and I was ready to be one of those multimillionaire real estate moguls dripping in diamonds and driving a Maybach, but first I have to go through this: chairs with kidney-shaped desktops attached and an instructor droning on for weeks and weeks. And there's no way out. In the Garden State, there's not only a state licensing requirement for real estate salespeople, there's also an attendance requirement. So for four weeks, no matter how smart you think you are, your butt goes in the desk and your eyes scan the linoleum.

I do Su Doku puzzles just to keep awake: the instructor's pretty good, but who can withstand four-and-a-half hours of agency law? (Think about *that* the next time you're shopping for a house: the "expert" salesperson driving you around was probably trying to figure out where the missing sevens went during a lecture on customer representation.)

There are 60 of us in class, one of the most diverse groups of people I can imagine: rich white moms looking for jobs that will let them flex their hours around their Matthews and Olivias; young black ghetto kids who saw an escape from their burger-slinging and hair-styling jobs after someone from the 'hood sold a house and started driving a new car; middle-aged immigrants from Portugal, Dominica, and Turkey who want to earn a little scratch by helping their friends settle in this big and confusing country.

I realize I have a huge advantage in school because I'm on the rich end of the spectrum. (I'm not dripping-in-diamonds rich, but I'm not flipping burgers either.) The poor kids ask questions that puzzle the suburbanites, questions that make the instructor cock his head to one side and speak extra s-l-o-w-l-y. We tend to segregate ourselves by color—which has happened in every classroom I've ever been in—but here the class line is an even bigger divider than the color line.

Many of the poor kids aren't stupid, but they don't know things about the way the rich people's world operates. So we'll talk about mortgages and they'll have all of these really basic questions. And why not? Some of these students have never even seen a mortgage statement.

When we wander into class discussion, we polo-shirt wearers share our droll tales of "It Happened to Me on Closing Day." The poor kids act like they're trapped on a deserted island with the Howells; they roll their eyes and wonder what the hell they've gotten into.

In one particularly painful interlude, the hair stylist (sporting brown braided extensions today; yesterday she was blonde) was trying to figure out what new career she was getting herself into. "How much do you get when you sell a house?" she asked.

"Well, it varies," said the instructor.

Now I know, that in the world of Foxtons and other discount brokers, he didn't want to say "6 percent." I also learned later, in a continuing education class, that whenever Realtors gather and talk about commissions, that's a possible antitrust violation. So he didn't want to say "6 percent" to a class he's training. (Apparently, for two non-Realtors to say "industry standard commissions are 6 percent, sliding down toward five" is fine, but for me to say it to you, if you've got your license, is fineable.)

The point is, the stylist wanted to estimate how much money she would make, and she didn't have the background to even guess. When she was growing up, she didn't hear dinner-table complaints about blood-sucking real estate agents and how they didn't deserve their 6 percent commission; she'd obviously grown up in a household where the adults were always trying to make the rent.

So she and the instructor went round-and-round for nearly 15 minutes: she wanted to budget for the first year of her career, and he wouldn't come straight out and answer her question. And I wondered about color and class. I wondered if I (highlighted blonde bob yesterday, highlighted blonde bob today) had posed the question, would the teacher have told me that some big franchises offer you a 50-50 split on the 3 percent you bring in as a buyer's broker, or that RE/MAX lets you keep their half of the split but charges $2,500 a month in desk fees?

I meant to catch up to her later and explain all this—I try to be friendly and helpful to everybody in class—but I never did. Honestly, I had good intentions, but I got too caught up in studying the linoleum.

Chapter 2

Learning to Drive

(Where Our Heroine Gets Asked for Heroin)

WHEN I STARTED my new life in real estate, it was based on a hand-shake with a New Jersey firm—they would fund my flipping venture and take two-thirds of the profits. We planned to concentrate on Newark, where home prices had been jumping 31 percent year-over-year. About a month into the adventure, we had agreed on an e-mailed business plan, but I was still waiting for the contracts with my partners to go through.

Though class had blessedly ended (the most torturous part was the extremely elementary math, which the engineer in the class had skipped on the grounds that she would shoot herself if she listened to someone work out the area of a triangle for two hours), I had nothing to do. I was eager to cruise around and shop for houses, but until I had contracts—and therefore funding—in place, I spent my time researching cars. It was not clear to me whether I'd be better off leasing (which would cost a couple hundred a month, plus as much for insurance and possibly more for parking) or getting a Zipcar.

And, of course, I had to learn to drive.

If you live most places in the United States, you may wonder how a person could possibly hit the advanced age of 38 without driving. The answer is a sad memory: when I was 15, my dad contracted Guillain-Barré, a rare and fast-acting paralytic disease (imagine multiple sclerosis hitting you in a week). No driver's seat for me; I spent months propped in a stiff plastic chair outside the intensive-care unit. Whenever I even think about driving, it brings back all that scary teenage powerlessness; other people smell burning rubber, I just get a faint and noxious memory of disinfectant.

I finally managed to get a license in Arkansas, where I grew up, by scooting around the block to the right, but in no way was I ready to pilot a car in the heavy urban traffic of New York or New Jersey. So now, every few days I'd make my way uptown for a driving lesson. (I'm taking classes not in Jersey, but in Manhattan, because I can get to them on the subway.)

Of all the obstacles I face—dishonest contractors, broken agreements, possible bankruptcy—I think the little red Nissan is the one that scares me most. The actual road time isn't that bad, really. It's a dual-brake car (the instructor reaches over and takes the wheel when he has to) and I get a bit less jagged every lesson. The driving school's philosophy is that if you learn in heavy city traffic, everything else will seem easy by comparison, so we cruise around Washington Heights and Harlem—areas with a lot of trucks, bikes, double-parked cars, and jaywalking pedestrians (which my Staten Island-raised husband refers to as "targets").

I'm painfully aware that my moves aren't automatic yet. It's like walking and going, "Okay, raise the right foot, now what comes down first, heel or toe?" Also, different teachers have different philosophies: one is happy to watch me ride my brake "just so long as you have control of the car" while another thinks it's a bad habit that will make me the cause of road rage forever.

A lot of cultural stuff is going on too—if you're not a New Yorker, let me explain that Washington Heights, with a large poor Dominican population, is starting to be gentrified by white yuppies. It's at once a vibrant neighborhood full of commerce and also the kind of place where a baby gets stabbed on the street. I read *The Bonfire of the Vanities* (okay, I know that was about The Bronx, but I'm still fearful). I stay on my guard; I don't want to have an accident here.

My newest and slickest driving teacher, Javier, is a Dominican kid who's about 20. As I get better at my left turns, I spend more time trying to eavesdrop on his cell phone conversations *en español*. But there's always culture shock: two little old ladies flagged us as we were parallel parking and asked us where they could *cenar*.

They want a restaurant, I thought, *I wonder where he'll send them around here?* It was only when he referred them to an *iglesia* that I realized they wanted a soup kitchen. Great—I'm worried about not bumping the curb with my tires, and these little gray-haired grandmothers don't have enough to eat.

Last week was the freakiest, though. We were on Broadway—a giant, multilane step forward—and these guys pulled up next to me and said, "Got any ... ?" Their accents were thick, the end of the question was unintelligible, and I looked over at Javi to do a *gringa* translation. He shook his head at them and told me to keep going.

As soon as we pulled away, he explained that they wanted to buy drugs. The driver had said, "Got any H?" meaning, "Got any heroin?" Of course, I thought, I'm in Harlem. I look like a peroxided Betty-fucking-Crocker and they think I'm selling heroin—or he is. Why else would a middle-aged white chick be up here in a car with a Dominican guy?

We laughed about that, Javi and I, and then the damn guys pulled up next to us again (Broadway's got a lot of stoplights). They said something else I couldn't translate. Frankly, I didn't catch it and didn't want to. I was so exasperated I cut off a small truck changing lanes to shake them. Instead of lecturing me, Javi smiled. "Nice job. Your driving is getting better."

Chapter 3

The Sheriff's Sale

(How Foreclosures Really Work)

WHEN I HAD been the real estate editor at the *New York Post,* I had cautioned my readers against buying any foreclosed home because they're like a box of chocolates—you never know what you're getting—and the average Joe can't handle surprises. But I thought maybe I could. I wanted to start flipping, and buying foreclosed homes is a classic flipper's strategy, so it seemed to me like the courthouse would be one of the obvious places to start.

Specifically, I had my eye on a house in Plainfield that I had seen listed as a foreclosure in the local paper. I still had no car, but I'd sauntered by the house (in that way that two bus rides and a half-mile on foot is a saunter). I thought that the outside, at least, looked remarkably well-kept.

So I landed at a sheriff's sale in Union County, New Jersey. According to foreclosure data providers RealtyTrac, one in every 1,215 households in New Jersey is in some stage of default; Union County (which includes towns like Roselle Park, Elizabeth, and Plainfield) is busy enough that there's a sheriff's sale every Wednesday. My flipping partners (the president, CEO, and COO of a realty firm, who I collectively called the Power Trio) wanted me to attend the sale to learn the lay of the land, although

SAVE YOUR HOME FROM FORECLOSURE

If you get behind in paying your mortgage, *you can lose your home.* If your payments are running late, make sure you take the following steps:

1. **Contact your lender.** Most delinquents ignore letters from the bank, hoping the problem will go away. Chances are it won't, but you have a better shot if you talk to your bank; they'd rather have money than take back your house.
2. **Contact an approved counselor.** A lot of potential home-buyers will offer foreclosure advice. For unbiased answers, go to the list of counselors approved by the U.S. Government Department of Housing: call toll-free 800-569-4287 or go to *www.hud.gov* and select "Foreclosure" from the left-hand bar.
3. **Negotiate a payment plan.** You can ask for a *cure* (a one-time 30-day grace from a missed payment) or set up a complete refinancing; just make sure you set up a plan to get out of the hole you're in.
4. **Keep records.** A November 2005 article by K. C. Camille in *Black Enterprise* magazine points out that you want to keep a record of every conversation you have with the bank, in case you end up in court. Write down the days and times when you chat, and get the name of everyone you talk to. Keep copies of your correspondence.
5. **Don't sign anything you don't understand.** An approved counselor should be able to hook you up with a lawyer who can explain documents to you; nothing that has to happen has to happen in a rush.

they hadn't authorized me to bid. "The other people at the sale are your competitors," the president had warned me. "Stay under the radar."

This was not even close to possible, because—*hello, I'm a chick.* Plus, like a rookie, I showed up on time, to be eyed by the Six Fat Guys, obviously regulars. Also, when they told us to turn off our cell phones, I was trying to seem neither reporter nor Realtor, but turning off *both* of my cell phones pretty much blew that cover.

Did I mention that I'm a chick?

The sale itself took place in a rectangular conference room/kitchen, the kind of place where a dozen people have meetings and twelve of them try to punch out their own eyeballs from the tedium. The room had a row of cabinets and a refrigerator along one long wall, a whiteboard on one end, and a long conference table in the middle. The whole thing was done in Danish Modern Fiberboard, from the cabinets to the table to the Eames-meets-Costco chairs that were ranged all around the edges of the room. Rest easy, Union County taxpayers: your public officials aren't wasting your money gussying up their conference rooms.

After passing through an ID/security checkpoint, people slowly filed in: young, muscled guys who stood lined up against the cabinets, newbies who sat scrunched in one end of the room, three female clerks who got to actually sit at the table. The Six Fat Guys dispersed themselves, some sitting at the end with the newbies but mostly plopping along the long wall facing the cute guys.

One of the Six Fat Guys started talking to a newbie: "A house in Westfield went for *one million dollars* in this very room," he said. "If I don't get this one, next time around I'm just going to go straight to the house, knock on the door, and say, 'hey, I'm going to make you a deal.'"

Then the sheriff's deputy walked in and the whole thing started (without, of course, any of the Latinate pronouncements I had imagined from watching Court TV). There's another bewilderment: houses are identified not by address but by case number. I'm lost. *They're talking about a house; which house? Is it my Plainfield house? What's going on?*

It sounded like a couple of houses got passed on completely—maybe the existing judgments against them are too high? I can't tell. Then bidding finally began on a property in Hillside. The cute guys started bidding

IF YOU WANT TO PLAY THE FORECLOSURE GAME

1. **Get some cash.** You're going up against contractors with a low cost of capital–their projects are often funded with cash out from under the mattress. Bring your own bag of money if you want to play.
2. **View the property.** Remember the current inhabitants are losing their home, and they usually aren't too kind to scavengers wanting to buy it. But you do want to know what you're getting into, and a knock on the door and a couple of fifties will sometimes get you in.
3. **Know that there aren't a lot of bargains.** In your head (or in some Learning Annex tapes) you may be thinking "30 percent off," but it's probably not going to happen. Thomas M. Carroll, Terrence M. Clauretie, and Helen R Neill of the University of Nevada–Las Vegas argued in the *Journal of Real Estate Research*

against each other in hundred-dollar increments, and as the price slowly rose, it dawned on me that they were contractors. (Attention singles: if you've ever wanted to snag a contractor, go to a foreclosure sale. In this room there's one hot Italian guy, one hot Portuguese guy, one hot Puerto Rican guy—it's like a bachelorette party at an auction.)

The bidding zipped between them for a while—*"one forty-four one* ($144.1K), *one forty-four two* ($144.2K), *one forty-five* ($145K), *one forty-five one* ($145.1K)"—and then there was a tidal shift as the price broke $200K. Turns out the contractors were just the undercard, and now the heavyweight bidders step into the ring: $291K from Ellis, $292K from Townsend. The bidding zooms by, and the house finally goes for $308.1K to Townsend.

It turns out we're done for the day. There were some two pages of sheriff's sales in the local paper (the Newark *Star-Ledger*) and they boiled down to bidding on just one house, that's it. It turns out the handling that foreclosures don't offer great discounts, so let me use their words: "If foreclosure, per se, results in such a large discount, we wonder why such properties were not purchased long before they made the multiple listing service. If real estate professionals handling these foreclosure sales do not recognize such profitable arbitrage prospects, who would?"

4. **Line up your repair team.** Every day the rehab clock is running costs you money. If you're a carpenter, make sure you've got a plumber to work with, and vice versa.

5. **Realize the home may not be yours outright.** Several states allow delinquent homeowners to buy back their property even after it's gone through foreclosure. Check with your lawyer to see if this property has such a *right of redemption* attached to it.

of "my" house got postponed, which is what happened to most of this batch.

I begin to glean more of the story of the sold Hillside house from what other people were saying as they left the room. "It's worth probably $350K," said one contractor who dropped out early.

"But you got to have a little wiggle room," said another. "He's a Realtor; he'll probably price it at $375K and sell it."

Certainly the winning bidder looked like he got a fab deal. If the repairs don't turn out to be extensive, he'll make what, $30,000? One of the few other nonclerk women in the room (his wife maybe?) was smiling and laughing with him, and other people in the auction were patting him on the back. "Well, Christmas is coming," he said to one. "And baby needs a new pair of shoes."

"And a coat," replied the other. Judging from the smile on the winner's face, it'll be coats for everybody.

But nobody forgot the contractor who dropped out early. One of the Six Fat Guys came up to him and thumped him hard on the back, too. "Congratulations," he said. "You lost again."

Chapter 4

Going Broke

(Precious Little Work, Worth Precious Little)

FALL 2005: I have my New Jersey real estate license. I go into my partners' office two or three days a week, and work on direct mail campaigns: *You don't have any money, please sell me your house for cheap so I can make some.* If you have ever gotten a postcard with an image of a guy holding hundred-dollar bills in his arms that says WE BUY HOUSES, you'll know what I'm talking about. The pieces I was writing were a step above that, but not by much.

Still, my direct mail generates a surprisingly high response rate. I had interviewed Mal Warwick, who is arguably the country's top guru on this stuff, and tried to take his lessons to heart: the customer doesn't care about the features of your hammer; the customer wants a nail in the wall. Still, once I get responses, I don't really know how to follow up on them. Sellers (the Power Trio president tells me never to call them *homeowners*; part of the real estate agent razzle-dazzle is that with a seller you never use the emotionally loaded word *home*) want a strong appreciation rate on their properties, and I just don't see how I can get those houses cheap enough. Also, some investment questions are quite complex: one girl wants me to sell her dad's lot, but my partners can't agree on whether it's buildable, and the people in the city offices in East Orange can't agree whether it's buildable, so I am terrified of paying $18,000 for a bunch of dirt that might turn out to be worthless. I trot to City Hall, where data is kept in books the size of tabletops and the air is as still as a library, but no one can make a definitive ruling for me and I can't get to the mayor. I go through city offices, maps, and zoning codes, but can't get reassurance from any one expert.

My October birthday (I'm 39) comes and goes. Ivan and I drive from Manhattan to West Point for a wedding, and I navigate the twisty Parkway in the rain, albeit at a the-other-drivers-hate-me nonspeed of 35 miles an hour. Then hubby and I have a ridiculously romantic dinner at Xaviar's, where we hold hands and talk seriously for the first time about maybe having kids, just as soon as this flipping venture works.

Then the climate gets chillier, and I start to get scared. Suddenly it's December, and four months after having quit my job (my precious job, with its blessedly steady paychecks), I learn that it isn't as simple as time equals money; it's that money also equals time.

I have always thought of my savings as providing me with a certain number of months where I don't have to make money flipping. At this point I had hoped to have six months of "video game" life left, and right now it looks more like four. *Four months! What have I done?*

When I quit my job, I had one strong force on my side: I'd done it before. I had freelanced in 1999 (during Web 1.0) and found it fairly easy to get magazine work for $1 or even a $1.50 a word and corporate work for $100 an hour. I worked for a bunch of publications then, and whenever I wanted to buy clothes, I'd write a corporate marketing piece.

Now it seems that there is no corporate work at all: I was hired by a Wall Street firm to do their PR for $100 an hour, with an estimate that they'd spend $2,000 a month, but the first time I billed them for $700 they freaked out. "Their expectations aren't right," suggested a friend of mine, a PR queen. "Drop 'em." So I did, but there's precious little to take their place: I have one gig, the column gig, and chasing everything else is tough and dispiriting.

When I first talked to my accountant about starting up this adventure, he noted that freelancers were generally doing well. "The person who trains my dogs makes a hundred dollars an hour," he said. Well, apparently writing is one of those services that has slipped down below dog training in the hierarchy. There's the story of the magazine that called me and commissioned a piece, simply on the strength of my previous work, had me do a first draft and then a rewrite and then killed the story without the editor-in-chief ever having read it: 50 hours, kill fee $350. The absolute low point came, I think, when one of my old writers referred me to a magazine that offered to pay me $40 per printed page—roughly 1/25th of what I made seven years ago.

The outflows, meanwhile, are staggering. When I made $90,000, my housing costs were killing me; now that I make less, it's almost unbearable. My husband feeds me, pays the $700 maintenance on the city apartment, and provides me with health insurance; but everything else—including the mortgage here in the city, medical care, and supporting the beach house that is my retirement plan—is up to me.

I later learned my struggles were generational—anybody under 40 should read Tamara Draut's fine book *Strapped* about why our generation is in such financial trouble—but political knowledge doesn't pay the bills. I try to keep my head above water, and in keeping with one of my gurus, Robert Shemin, I try very hard to stay home on Fridays and "run my business"—not just look for houses to flip, not just look for work, but contemplate the big picture. One component of this is to do a basic cash flow statement. Here's what a sample month from the fall might look like:

Income: (Column, misc. writing work, rent): $3,500
Outgo: $8,100
   Mortgage (beach): $1,630
   Mortgage (city): $1,450
   Prorated taxes, beach: $750
   Shrink: $750
   House insurance: $200
   HELOC interest: $100
   Heat:
   (this number got worse as it got colder) $400
   Nonheat utilities
   (electric, cable, Internet, telephones, water): $350
   Transport
   (includes train, car rental, taxis, driving lessons): $350
   Big business expenses
   (law services, real estate classes, etc.): $200
   Small business expenses
   (stationery, Realtor dues, photocopying, printing,
   computer time at Kinko's): $200
   Entertainment
   (generally buying someone smarter than me lunch
   for their advice): $125
   Gym: $100
   Gardener (try running a rental without one): $75
   Credit card interest: $100
   Credit card paydown: $200
   Clothes/hair: $100
   Small house repair (say, a window replacement): $200
   Cash withdrawals
   (for services that need to be paid in cash, like contractors,
   tips, birthday gifts; petty cash for buying bread, milk,
   and shampoo on the way home): $820
Burn: $4,600

To save you the trouble of looking for what isn't there, I haven't paid any income or Social Security taxes on the freelancing yet.

In my head, it's $5,000 a month more than I make, and I haven't yet made some necessary repairs at the beach house (looks like this girl's getting a new roof for Christmas). Woo hoo, I'm losing $60,000 a year!

I'm stressed, I worry, and I cry, and I can see the concern in the eyes of my friends. My friend Joyce at *The New York Times* reads my columns and sends me notes of concern. "I worry about you," she writes. It's getting tougher to get up in the morning, and my darling husband is developing little frowny lines on his face.

Chapter 5

Media Inc.

*(My Rich Client with the Jaguar Shops for a
Summer Home)*

THE POWER TRIO keeps sending me contractors to interview so that
when I do find a property we think will be suitable for flipping, the contractors will be in place. I can sort them into two categories: white contractors, who consider the areas of Newark and the Oranges I am looking at "too dangerous" and won't work there, and nonwhite contractors,
mostly Latin Americans, who keep cash in their safe-deposit boxes and
would buy any really good flip for themselves. How can I compete with
these guys, whose cost of capital is lower than mine, because they haven't
paid taxes on their money? I shove that thought to the back of my mind,
but it's early December, and the prospect of running out of money in
March is still terrifying; it seems so close. So I start to develop yet another
line of business: being a buyer's rep.

This, to me, seems very much like my old job—I have to use my research skills to come up with a huge haystack of information, and then dig
through it to find the needle that makes a cranky rich person happy. My
first assignment comes about accidentally—I heard a Big Media Executive
speak, wrote him an e-mail saying I liked his speech, and could I buy him
lunch? It turned out he wanted a summer rental in the Jersey hills.

After pointing out the very happy coincidence that I actually had a license to go hunting for Jersey rentals, I asked why he didn't already have a summer place. "I e-mailed a bunch of Realtors once," Big Media Exec said. "But nobody called me back."

So I vowed, first, to be the calling-backest person he'd ever met. (Hell, I have four months to live.) I jumped out of my looking-for-a-flip mufti and into a pinstriped suit and pumps: I looked a little '80s-investment-banker, but trustworthy. We had a lovely lunch in the city at One Madison Park, watching flights of wine come and go at the tables around us, and I listened to exactly what he wanted. Then, I implemented a rule that has served me well in journalism: when you're in trouble, make 10 phone calls.

Most news stories these days are reported off the basis of three phone calls, and if you know a housing market really well—in terms of what inventory is available and what inventory's probably going to be available—you can probably find a client a home in three calls as well. But I was too inexperienced for that, so I called 10 agents.

I found one problem. Apparently they don't do summer rentals in Jersey, except on Long Beach Island (too shore-y for us) and at a couple of lake communities my client would consider too *déclassé*.

So of the 10 agents I called, only four called me back. At least I lined up three showings for my client. Then, the second challenge (and I know this one from journalism, too) was shutting up.

Here's Big Media Exec—he rubs elbows with what I'd call first-name celebs, people I watch on TV. And I'm bursting with questions: *How much money does my favorite celeb make? What's Martha really like? Who's nasty and who's nice? Can Big Media Exec make me a star?*

None of these, unfortunately, are askable questions. We drove around Jersey in his Jag, and I admit I fawned when presented with that obvious toy, an $80,000 sports car. I felt that good taste prevented me from asking the pressing question: *What's it like to have sex in an auto that cost more than my first home?* I settled for drifting into a cone of silence whenever he was on his cell phone (which was most of the time before and after the showings).

Part of my role-playing was shaped by my own experiences of driving around with real estate agents; I've found their constant nattering about this restaurant and that tennis club just made my head hurt. I tried to remember the style of Gil Neary, the DG Neary broker who sold me my first two co-ops; Gil would tell me something about a building, and then fade into the background while I reacted to it. I realize now that what he was doing was *listening,* and I tried to imitate it.

At the same time, I tried a third business tactic: infusing the house-hunt with a spirit of adventure. We were looking for a summer rental to be a surprise Christmas present from Big Media Exec to his wife—sweet, no? So I started trying hard to make sure that romantic impulse spilled over into the shopping itself. Every house we saw, we made up a narrative of the people who must have lived there before, guessing who made the decision that caused each room to look the way it did.

Most of the stuff we saw was pretty junky—historic, but never updated. I also learned that my client has a slight phobia about dogs, a bit tricky for someone who is looking for property in the country. And always, there's the pressure of his work: a call that has to be taken so that the country's media wheels can move and the rest of us get our comedy and cooking tips. After one particularly hairy call that sounds like it saves a megastar a couple of million, my client turns to me and says, "Now do you understand why I need a retreat?"

So we persevere and find a rental that I think he'll take. It's a nineteenth-century Grand Old House that's been ruined by some coke dealer with no sense of history. It has all-marble bathrooms with cathedral ceilings and bidets, a wreck of a kitchen, and mirrors on the master bedroom ceiling(!). But the fireplaces and the moldings are still there, and it could be cleaned up by someone with appropriately Georgian sensibilities.

FIVE THINGS TO ASK BEFORE YOU RENT A VACATION PROPERTY

1. Am I renting everything I see? Are linens (sheets, towels, tablecloths) provided? Are there pieces of furniture or other items I see now (such as a set of dishes or a stereo) that will be locked away or not included in the rental?
2. Do you already have a cleaning person? How often does he or she come, and is this service included in the rental cost?
3. What's parking like during the high season? Is there parking attached to the property I'm renting? What about at the beach or tennis club? Do I need some kind of club or municipal permit, and how do I get it?
4. Are there neighboring dogs or cats that have access to the property? Can I bring my dog or cat? Do you have trouble with deer, snakes, raccoons? Are there tick or Lyme disease problems?
5. I came here to get back to nature ... so where's the movie theater? Even though your goal may be "to get away from it all," don't forget to ask about bits of civilization you may want. Where's the pizza parlor? Liquor store? Place to buy a big-city newspaper?

What's more, it has a steep and twisty driveway. That's romantic; in the summer, it will be perfectly fine for the two little kids to run down and for the $80,000 sports car to make its way up. But every time my client looks at it, he'll remember instead slipping in the snow in his city shoes, nearly breaking his neck so he could find just the perfect gift to put under the tree for the one he loves.

There's just one problem with wrapping up the house: the owner doesn't really want to rent it out. I'd forgotten the pull of romance on the other side: the owner, a recent widower, has listed the property as a rental without necessarily intending to let go of it. There's a mish-mosh of furniture, but the place isn't ready for a family. We ask for it to be furnished, and the owner says no; there's a marble dining table that seats eight, the kind of sharp-cornered thing that you don't want little kids around, and the owner says he has no intention of moving it.

I'm desperate; I need a deal. I call up a furniture rental place in the city and get a quote for what it would cost to load up the place with queen beds and dressers and end tables and what have you. I know my client has his heart set on "a really big TV" that he described with the hand motions that you make when you're describing a 60" flat-screen. You can't really rent one of those, as far as I can figure out, but I run the numbers with the cost of the furniture included and point out what a bargain it is, compared to the Hamptons. I even offer to buy and throw in a TV, although on my budget I think we're looking at a 42" old-fashioned set.

My client is adamant, NO. You don't get to be Big Media Exec by letting people jack you around, and vacation rentals should come with furniture; it's not the money, it's the principle of the thing.

It's not the money; it's the sands in the hourglass that I fear. I want to make a deal while my client is still enamored, before he gets distracted by something else. Then, a slight opening: the owner lets it be known that he'd put the house on the market for sale, but he won't name a price. I feel like Power Trio president lets me down here; the way to value a house is to look at comparable houses, but I have no experience with nearby fancy towns like Peapack and Gladstone, and thus little idea how to comp out a $2.5 million house. (The listing agent, bless her heart, helps me out here, and she and I go back and forth arguing about which recently sold houses are applicable as comps.)

So I sit in the office and I struggle, looking out on the parking lot and trying to imagine what would make Big Media Exec happy. He's in love with the property, and suggests that we just "make an offer," clearly overlooking the fact that I've never written a contract in my life, that he would need a weird mortgage structure because he doesn't want to put any money down, and that we would only be guessing how much money the owner wants, because we don't have a listing price to anchor us.

One of my Wall Street friends suggest that if you were a financial wizard you could probably get a Wall Street bank to lend you a couple of million as a loan against stock options, and I figure my friend has plenty of those. But I just don't have the social connections to call my friend Richie over at Fancy Bank Co. and ask him to outline such of thing for the sake of an old squash buddy. It looks at one point like it will all coalesce anyway, somewhere around $2.4M, and then the owner decides it's worth *five million,* hooker bathrooms and all.

I get a Christmas card from Big Media Exec, but he kind of drifts away, failed by yet another real estate agent. I hope his wife got a nice bracelet for Christmas.

Chapter 6

Cramped

(An Outline of My Predicament)

OH, THE JOYS of starting a new business. We're cramped, we're going broke, and I don't know how—or when—to fix it.

In some ways I miss space more than money. I don't really have a place to work: in Jersey, I'm on desk share, so I keep being shuttled around as more senior agents show up to claim "their" desks. The COO cleaned out one file drawer for me, so I have a place to stick a coffee cup, but in just a couple of months I've already got it about a third full with files. And of course, I'll have to pick up some freelance work, and some of my columns are reported, which leads to the working-at-home problem.

My home office is a room 14 feet by 24 feet, about the size of a suburban American living room. Not a bad size, but the problem is, I have to sleep there too. And eat, and keep all my stuff, and my husband's stuff (did I mention 14×24 is way too palatial for one person?).

So here's the layout of our entire home: Off the studio is a walk-in closet, five feet by eight, which we converted to a den just so we could have separate rooms and a door to slam between them. We call the converted closet the Nook. There's a love seat, and some CDs and books, and a TV. No window, of course, but it's still a godsend for when one of us, usually me, wants to sleep early and the other wants to stay up watching TV. Sure, hubby complains that it's airless, and a federal white-collar prison cell would actually be bigger (six feet by eight), but we make do.

Then there's a bathroom (tub, toilet, sink, no window) and a kitchen (dishwasher, sink, stove, fridge).

The stuff that normal people would have put in the walk-in closet goes in the coat closet, three feet by three feet, which houses Ivan's clothes, my coats, the wrapping paper and the vacuum, or it goes in the five foot by six foot dressing room, which houses my clothes and our folding chairs for guests and all the household linens.

That's it, there isn't any more. We're lucky because I bought this a few years ago, before Midtown went crazy, so it costs us only $2,000 a month to live here. If we sold it now, we'd get a shade over half a million.

Yes, you read that right.

The main room has a lot of furniture wedged into it, and it's not bad when we're both gone all day. There's a Murphy bed with bookcases, the best purchase we ever made, and a china cabinet for our wedding stuff and an entertainment center with the TV. There's a tall cabinet for writing supplies, and two for files, and one for keys. There's a sofa and a coffee table, and two comfy club chairs and side tables. The Mixmaster, the off-season clothes, more books, all my old writing clips, and grandma's heirloom chair are all in storage—four units in three ZIP codes—but we've kept with us quite a lot of stuff.

It's great until you have to work there. As I write this, I'm eating dinner at my desk, which is also my coffee table; there's no desk in this apartment, and I wrote most of this book sitting on my living room floor. When my back really gives out I'll put the laptop on my husband's dresser or my dresser, for height variation, but there's nowhere to put my knees and I keep getting hit in the head by my sweaters. The visual clutter is insane, because the filing cabinets are stuffed to the gills, and the house is full of little heaps of unfiled mail and bills and source material, some of it in manila folders in orderly piles on the china cabinet, but some of it just out. A business card lands in this apartment and it looks cluttered. (Memo to everyone: Stop sending me things!) Plus, I'm my own plant service, and I must say, the begonias look crappy.

Outlet space is also at a huge premium, which is a problem because my laptop battery is dead and it must be plugged in to work. Last night I woke up Ivan when I pulled the computer's power supply away from the power strip with the lamp, the digital camera recharger, his cell-phone recharger, my cell-phone recharger (work), and the white noise machine to move the power supply into the Nook to put it into the power strip with the TV, one of the DVRs, the iPod charger, the stereo receiver, the DVD player, and my cell-phone recharger (home). I guess if I bomb in the real estate biz I can always start an electronics resale store.

I remember great offices I've been in: that of my friend who runs a gazillion-dollar hedge fund, a steward-of-Capitalism trophy office with a commanding view of Central Park; Lou Gerstner's as CEO of IBM, where he had two anterooms and a wine refrigerator; those of kingpin real estate developers, with maps of the blocks of Miami they own; and the vice chairman of Donaldson, Lufkin & Jenrette's, with an Alex Katz painting hung where a normal person would put a poster, and I just sigh. Nuns, the poet says, fret not at their convent's narrow room. But I'm no nun, and I fret at mine a lot.

Chapter 7

A Wreck of a House
at Christmas

(What the Crack Addicts Left Behind)

Sleigh bells ring, are you listening?
(from "Winter Wonderland" by Smith and Bernard)

MY PARTNERS' FIRM has a Christmas party, which I find out about kind of late, but I am so excited. *I get to meet everybody. I get to explain my whole flipping deal.* There will be meatballs, I'll do a quick speech, and I'll smile—and it will be like Moses at Sinai: the word will go out. Not that I'm being grandiose or anything, but I'm excited.

Better that I not be: just as I'm asked to speak, I'm told not to say anything about the flipping venture. "Just in case somebody else gets jealous," Power Trio CEO says. Rather than make a big announcement about the rehab initiative (and therefore wound the feelings of whichever agents might have felt like they wanted to lead it) the partners simply introduce me as the *Post* girl, wringing some credibility out of my credentials but not letting me advance my agenda.

I'm angry at being wrong-footed, but I'm adaptable. Hey, when in corporate life was I ever allowed to lead through strength and openness? Making my way by degrees is what I'm good at. When I next go into the office, I decide I will tell the agents one by one what I'm up to. The first thing I do is sit down at my desk and start eavesdropping. I'm not terribly proud of it, but an agent in my office was telling an investor about a too-new-to-be-listed rehab. And so I raised my hand: "If he doesn't want it, I want it."

This agent, luckily, was a strong producer who was pretty secure, and didn't care who the buyer was as long as he got the best price for his client. The client was in a hurry, he said, so we went to see the house the next day.

It was a three-story, three-family in the South Ward of Newark—an area famous for its race riots four decades ago, but slowly stabilizing now. Half the houses on the street were boarded up, while half had new doors or siding or some other sign of love and care. I figured the area looked junky, and it didn't look white, but even though I would stick out like a sore thumb, I could work in it. (Not everyone shared my attitude; later, when the COO's wife came by to see it with us, she wouldn't even get out of the car.)

Our target house was in the boarded-up half. It was the first time I had ever seen shrouded padlocks, where the lock itself is encased in a little weather-proof, bolt-cutter-proof shell. These fastened a sheet of plywood on three sides, so getting in was like entering a little kid's clubhouse: after the agent snapped the locks off, he swung the plywood upward, and we duck-walked in from the side.

The house was pitch dark. Duh! Where's the light in a boarded-up house supposed to come from? We switched on our lanterns—serious mineworkers' jobs that are a little too pro to be called *flashlights,* and went through the house. (We yelled, "Realtors, Realtors" just to be on the safe side; Newark has to be the only place where saying that *won't* get you shot.)

I write weekly dispatches about my real estate adventures, which I had pitched as "trading in my Jimmy Choos for a hard hat," and this is the first time in four months life really feels that way. *Hey, I'm in the belly of the flip.* What's it like? Well, your intrepid heroine is playing a beam of light through a darkened house, and she sees ... crap everywhere. Abandoned mattresses, fast-food wrappings, in one case actual human waste where someone had squatted like a dog over a piece of plastic, and then wandered off again. I feel only drugs could have caused people to live like this. I had seen a crèche proudly displayed on someone's lawn the day before, and what stuck in my head was, "I wonder if conditions in the manger were this bad." At one point, my partner moved a refrigerator, and a yowl and a streak of escaping black-and-white fur revealed that he'd surprised a cat. Frankly, I was glad it wasn't some kind of gigantor rat.

The situation was just shocking. I was so moved by walking through this house that later, I wrote a column about it, lamenting that people lived in such dreadful conditions. In response, I got letters; wonderful, warm, caring letters, from a bunch of readers who wanted to make sure that the kitty cat was all right.

Interestingly enough, this sordid wreck of a house didn't smell bad, it just looked bad—cleanup needed here, falling plaster there; let's see, how much would 40 new windows cost?

Was it only two months ago I was talking to flipper Steve Berges about the magic of carpet and paint? (For his comments, see page 182.) This place needed carpet and paint, plus cleanup with a dumpster, new siding, new windows, a new heating system, three new kitchens, and three new baths. Power Trio president guessed $70,000, but said we needed to bring in a general contractor to get a more formal repair cost estimate.

The listing agent, of course, cast the place in the best possible light, explaining that each floor was a separate flat, and that you could put an Ikea closet in each of the house's three dining rooms, making each unit qualify as a Section 8-approved three-bedroom. With $70,000 of repair costs, it might have worked; the nice, hardworking people who had to live next to this eyesore probably paid $300K for each of their houses. But there turned out to be two problems: first, the owner had paid $190K and wanted to recoup his investment (although one doubts that when he bought it that it was such a literal shithole), and second, was the problem of GCs—general contractors. The nice Irish guy the firm had introduced me to said he wouldn't even work in the neighborhood; why risk a truck full of tools? The Ecuadorians seemed too expensive, and that left us with the old black guy, who looked me straight in the eye and told me that for me, he could do it for $150K. Let's see: $190K purchase plus $150K rehab costs to get a $300K house ...

It was starting to dawn on me, oh so slowly, that maybe this was not going to work.

Chapter 8

A New Year's Wish

(Meditations on the Death of Two Jersey Cops)

HAPPY NEW YEAR, dear readers!

It's wonderful to be able to write a New Year's column. Every columnist looks forward to the holidays as a chance to write a "perennial"—a column that takes the concerns of the present and mixes them up with more important and more spiritual themes. You know, like, "Yes, Virginia, there is a Santa Claus."

So of course the natural thing to do is to put forth a series of New Year's resolutions that are at once witty and reflective and insightful and charming. But I can't do that, because I can't stop thinking about those Jersey cops.

Here's the story I read in the *Star-Ledger:* There's a drawbridge that goes over the Hackensack River, linking Jersey City and Kearney. The middle section gets raised every now and then to let boat traffic through; normally, mechanical barriers keep traffic from going forward when the bridge is raised, but recently a traffic accident took them out. So the past few times they've had to raise the bridge, the bridge operators have called Kearney cops, and they've set up flares to stop traffic.

On Christmas Day, for some reason, the bridge operators called cops on the Jersey City side instead. Maybe they wanted to give the Kearney cops a holiday; maybe it was the guys from Jersey City's turn, I don't know. Anyway, two cops got into their car, drove over the bridge to the Kearney side, and delivered the flares that would signal that the bridge was raised. It was terrible weather apparently, with chaos pouring down from the skies: a heavy fog and rain coming down in sheets.

Despite the weather, the cops delivered their flares, and then turned right back around and drove over the no-longer-there bridge. These two good guys, with 22 years of service between them, plunged some 40 feet into icy water, to their deaths. On Christmas.

The tabloids had a hard time with this story, because it's okay to have brave cops, or corrupt cops, or even foolish cops, but it's absolutely not okay to have dead bird-brained cops. Any cop who dies in the line of duty is by definition a hero, and you can't snigger at him or her. After all, dear reader, your turn too will come, and who knows but that you might not choke to death on a ham sandwich or strangle yourself in the changing room at Saks?

As 2005 turned into 2006, I was obsessed by this story because it was both tragic and comic. I saw it as a parable about The Path—even when you are lighting the way for others, you have to pay attention to the road for yourself. You have to focus constantly on where you're going and how you're going to get there. And that's a valuable thing to think about at New Year's, when each of us takes time to ponder his or her road (even if you only go as far as vowing to be 10 pounds lighter walking down it).

I have a vision that the real estate industry can be less mystifying and bureaucratic than it currently is, and that some ramshackle city neighborhoods can be brought back with care, house by house, and that while I am changing my little corner of the world I can make enough money to have a couple of kids. That's my path and I believe in it, strongly.

Oh Lord, let there be a bridge.

Chapter 9

The Lowball Offer

(Trying to Knock a Seller into Reality)

IT'S JANUARY 2006, and the bloom might be coming off the rose. A picture may be worth a thousand words, but nobody's house is worth what they think it is in this market.

The tough part is telling people that.

I went to see a house in Southwest Newark, practically in Hillside, in an area where the neighborhood changes drastically from block to block. I went at night, which on reflection was slightly stupid, but I didn't know that part of town well and was trying to get a handle on what the city was like. (I have always held to the "eat your own cooking" philosophy.) I haven't been able to afford a car, so I took a bus and then walked along for a while, watching respectable blocks alternate with loud blocks and deserted blocks by turn.

Then I came to what can only be called a nice block, with tiny little Colonials in decently kept rows. We're talking small houses—1,800-square-foot, three bedrooms, with Ma and Pa and the kids sharing just one bath—but they're great starter homes. There was a listing of one house for $199K, which was described in the MLS as a "rehab" candidate (in the remarks the agent wrote, "under market price").

PUTTING IN A LOWBALL OFFER

A question I get all the time from potential buyers is: "How low can I go?" They always ask this in the abstract, as though there's one number that's the absolute answer and I can somehow tell them over the phone, roughly like calling your doctor and saying, "Hey, I think I'm having a mild stroke, which medicine should I take?"

But in general, there is a zone where your offer is insultingly low. Some investment theorists strategize that that's okay, go ahead and make ridiculous offers, as long as you're willing to ask a gazillion people until you find the tired one who will capitulate. Then it's like you won the lottery.

I don't generally think that's true. For one thing, anybody so broke that they might actually face losing their house is so broke that bankruptcy's a viable option. Anybody else is probably going to have a middle-class sense of money and entitlement, and they're probably going to think their house is worth way more than it is.

So let's think of pricing like a football field, and let's think of two possible strategies: one where you start really far away, and you're just tossing a Hail Mary, and if it fails you expect never to hear from the seller again, and one where you want to engage the seller in a pricing dialogue—to move the line of scrimmage, as it were.

My 30 percent off asking was an absolute Hail Mary—and it didn't work. The only circumstances where it probably would are where 1) the seller has absolute time pressure, such as an impending move, and 2) the house is so overpriced that you're really only fleecing the seller by about 10 percent. Try to get a larger discount than that, and you'll find the seller starts to think that renting the property out ain't such a bad option.

If you want to engage the seller, it will help to know a factor called *negotiability* or *discount*. (I have to give credit here to economist Jonathan Miller of Miller Samuel, a New York City appraisal firm, for being the first to introduce me to the term.) Negotiability is the average spread between what houses list for and what they sell for. If a house is listed at $500K and sells for $475K, its negotiability was 5 percent. The stat tells buyers where sellers expect to end up.

Informed buyers then have a choice of two positions: the first is to come in very close to the negotiability range, and subsequently dig in their heels. You listed at $500K, negotiability is 5 percent, therefore implicitly you're expecting $475K; I'm going to bid $470K, and I'm going to tell you that's the best I can do. Will that work? Depends on how much of a hurry the seller's in, whether they think they have a house with above-average marketability, and what their other offers have been like.

If the buyer comes in much lower than the negotiability implies, the seller assumes they're going to "split the difference"—which means that I assume you want to end up halfway between your first bid and my listing price. I list at $500K, you bid $420K; I'm going to hear that as dictating that you want to get the house for $460K, and evaluate it accordingly.

So that's the rough idea; of course there are as many refinements as football coaches have for run and pass plays. That's why you hire a professional negotiator. Dispassion counts for a great deal too, which is why people who negotiate for a living, such as lawyers and salespeople, may be good at going back and forth and yet generally should not negotiate their own deals.

What if you must try this at home—i.e., put in a lowball offer without using an agent? In general, if a seller is in a 5 percent negotiability market, she's hoping for a bid of 10 percent off list so she can ask you to split the difference, and then sit around and eat bonbons. If you're buying, and you put in a bid of 15 percent off list, it probably won't make the seller wince, though if she's in a position of strength she'll ignore it. Put in a bid of 20 percent off list, and the seller won't regard you as worth engaging in negotiations with. Unless she has pressing cash needs, you will have blown your shot.

But maybe that's your strategy, to put in a lot of lowballs. If you feel like you have other targets to shoot at, then that's just fine.

Well, she got half of that right. To say the house was a rehab candidate was putting it mildly—it had a '70s kitchen, carpet that needed replacing, holes that needed to be patched in the plaster ceilings of every room, and it was just begging for paint. In addition, there was junk everywhere. Walk in, and you entered through a narrow hall made narrower by the winter coats hung up on both sides. You could squeeze past them, but bits of cloth and down brushed your shoulders. It felt like entering Narnia.

Full market price for a house that size in that neighborhood, according to the comps, was $210K. Throw in a little "everybody loves Newark" fudge factor and that would bring you up to $225K for something with paint. So this house was no bargain.

I tried to prepare the homeowner for this as I toured the house with her. "The new construction across the street is going for nearly $500K," she said to me.

"Yes," I said. "Those new-builds look nice, but they're three-family houses with rental incomes attached."

"We put in an extra half-bath in the basement," she said.

"Yes, but it might have to be redone," I argued.

And so we went, back-and-forth. She insisted that her husband was "getting around to" patching the plaster ceilings, and I gently suggested that there were few handymen around of the generation that could decently dovetail that repair. (Often, when you see a smooth flat ceiling in an old house, it's because it was easier to put drywall over a hole in the plaster than to find a skilled plasterer from the Old Country.)

The homeowner, I mean the house owner, was living in what the speculators refer to as a POS: a piece of shit. But she didn't see her house as a POS, as worn or even shabby; she saw a home where she'd spent 11 Thanksgivings and was sad to leave.

I liked her so much that as I left I made one suggestion to her.

"It needs some work; it'll show better if you take the coats out."

Then I waited a couple of days, mulling, and called the seller's agent.

"Look," I said. "I know she's been in that house for a long while, and she's sad to be moving, but it's barely worth $199K new. To rehab it, I've got to put in a new kitchen, revamp the bath, polish up from top to bottom where it hasn't been taken care of. It looks like it's got no major structural defects, but I've still got to put $40,000 into it."

The seller's agent didn't even bother to argue that a new kitchen and bath and carpet might not cost $40,000 (and to tell the truth, I didn't know, because I didn't do the walk-through with a contractor; I was leaving myself some wiggle room).

"So you're offering ... what?"

"One-forty. I don't want to insult the owner because she was so nice, but she just doesn't understand what a dumpy condition the house is in. If she can fix it up and get her price, power to her, but if it sits, remember me; I'm her backup offer."

I went over this story with one of my partners, Power Trio COO. I'm still pretty new at making offers, and I wanted him to hear every detail of the story, see the house as I saw it, and be an audience to my conversation with the agent.

He had only suggestion: "Don't be apologetic. Not, 'I'm sorry, but I can only offer you one-forty,' but, 'My offer's one-forty.' You don't know what she's thinking and how she'll handle it. That's it, 'One-forty.'"

Useful words—but I wasn't optimistic about this one. And indeed, I never heard back.

Chapter 10

The Estate Section House

(Tricks to Keep from Overpaying)

FINALLY, A HOUSE I don't need to carry a weapon to walk into.

A little background: I have not been getting enough leads. I went to work for this Jersey firm to get leads from their network, and I've still been floundering around like I'm doing this alone.

It turns out that's because I am doing this alone. Those mysterious contracts I've never seen? It would have done me well to see them, because it turns out that my "I provide the skill, they provide the capital" arrangement isn't with my firm, it's with the partners in my firm.

Oh. *Shit.*

Well, I'm halfway through the tunnel now, and I might as well see what's on the other side. After pleading with the Power Trio's president, he did something I hoped he would do four months ago—put me in front of the salespeople.

The idea was that I could tell them what I was looking for, and maybe one of their listings would work. Or maybe someone would come across a property that would be just the thing. That's what all the real estate investing books say to do: get the word out that you're looking for deals. Better to have dozens of pairs of eyes searching for you than to rely on your wits alone.

So I made up little flyers for all the salespeople in the home office, stating what I was trying to do. And I'll say it again, because maybe I'll convince myself: I want to do rehabs of reasonably priced-homes because I think the middle class needs (and deserves) decent housing. I feel like if this fails, I'll become just another New York City broker chasing $2 million listings. And I'm sure that would be a fun job, but it doesn't feel like a mission.

Anyway, on my flyers I told all the salespeople what I was looking for, and that I would need a $70,000 spread between the price I could get the home for, and the price I could sell it for after it was fixed-up.

I only got one bite, but it was from an agent who supplied me with three different MLS sheets—three properties from our multiple listing service database. She must have missed the $70,000 part, though.

Sheet 1 was for a property in East Orange; I know East Orange pretty well, and this was too fully priced to rehab and still make money. Sheet 2 was for a property in Irvington, a town I don't know. And Sheet 3 was for this cute little Colonial in the estate section of Orange. It was listed at $389K, and homes all around it were typically selling in the $500Ks. *Woo hoo!*

I showed the sheet to the head of my firm. "It's too expensive," he said. "Take a look but there's no room to rehab it."

When I waved the $500K comp at him, he dismissed it. "The house for sale is smaller. You can't just say, 'this is three bedrooms and that is three bedrooms, so they're comparable.' You've got to count the front windows."

You know what? He was right.

The house was probably built in the nineteen-teens, and it was limited by its bathrooms. The main floor had a living room, dining room, and a porch that had been enclosed to make a baby's room. The kitchen was too small (by today's standards), with only a few feet of counter space, and the only way to make it bigger would have been to bust through a powder room, which would eliminate the only bath on that floor.

The upstairs had a master and two smaller bedrooms, all sharing one bath. That was a problem too: if you're a first-time buyer shopping for a

TRICKS TO KEEP FROM OVERPAYING

There's a saying in real estate: "You make money when you buy, not when you sell." Here are five tips to keep in mind:

1. **Run comps on the home several different ways:** by what similar layouts cost, by what homes of similar ages cost, by price per square foot. My friend Lena was really excited about a Carroll Gardens apartment—a two-bedroom, two-bath condo that was priced in line with other two-bedroom, two-bath condos—until I pointed out that the per square foot price was *$50 more* than anything else on the market.

2. **The minute you fall in love, find a backup.** You won't bid into the stratosphere to get your dream place if you've already lined up another you like almost as much. Front Porch motto: There's always another house (or another apartment).

3. **Repeat your offer.** Dian Hymer wrote a piece on Inman News *(www.inman.com)* in May 2006 pointing out that it can take sellers a little while to adjust to a cooling market—but sometimes when you say "that's my best and final" they come around.

4. **Make sure you love the neighborhood, not the property.** No matter how glamorous your target home is, it will age; in 20 years, you'll have to update even the most state-of-the-art kitchen and baths. But location, location …

5. **Consider improving the terms of your offer rather than the amount.** The Redfin blog *(blog.redfin.com)* posted a story of a couple that won a bidding war in Boston by offering the relocating seller four months' free housing at their place in California. While "hey, be my roommate" is a bit extreme, you might want to consider increasing your down payment or putting the closing on the seller's timetable.

house, and you can drop $500K, you can actually get a master bath these days.

So the upshot was, it was a small cute house in a great neighborhood. It was worth $425K, *if* it was mint mint mint. But what stood between me and that $425K was a new kitchen and two new baths and a new door and about 20 new windows. Oh, and paint, did I mention paint? I'd have to do a perfect job to hit that comp.

The original list was at $445K. According to the selling broker, the owner really, really thought it was worth that. I floated the idea of offering $320K and was told to put it writing. "But it probably won't fly," the selling broker said.

The secret reason was that there wasn't that much equity in the house. I didn't think about this when I started (oh, there's a lot I didn't think about when I started) but one of the principles of flipping is that you've got to buy houses cheaply. And one of the reasons you can buy houses cheaply, the thinking goes, is that when house values have been rising, sellers will still walk away with a nice little paycheck.

In truth, as house values have been rising, sellers have been treating their houses like ATMs, taking out second mortgages and HELOCs (home equity lines of credit) like the family home is just another cash machine. I'm guilty of this too—I had thrown a HELOC onto my beach house to finance this silly venture.

Now if all the equity in a house has been cannibalized, a seller can't sell cheap. Let's say the mortgages on this puppy total $300K, and then the salesperson takes $20,000, is the seller going to accept a mere $320K? Is she going to take $340K, or is she going to hang on for a year in hopes that someone stupider than me comes along?

Well, if you've been reading along, you know the answer to that: there ain't no one stupider than me.

Chapter 11

The "Come to Jesus" Letter

(Sometimes You Just Have to Punch Somebody in the Nose)

FOUR MONTHS INTO my New Jersey adventure, things were not working as I'd hoped. I still had no contract with my flipping partners; worse, I still had no connections.

Because a lot of new development was going on in East Orange, I had picked it as an area to concentrate on. In the fall, the Power Trio had told me that I would meet the mayor of East Orange "before the end of the year"—that time came and went without my even getting an appointment.

So as part of a New Year's WTF program, I had lunch with one of my friends in New York, the CEO of a smallish brokerage firm. He's a pretty busy guy, but I figured if anyone could be an elder statesman about this whole situation, he could.

We went to our favorite sushi place, and he told me mournfully he thought the whole flipping thing was just a dumb idea. "Why don't you just sell real estate?" he asked. "It's easier than flipping, and you know going into the deal what your margin will be."

I mentioned that I was, indeed, thinking of taking my license in New York, but I also needed part-time work—I was stunned at how little freelance work I was getting—and that I was reluctant to leave my partners because it always seemed like something was just around the corner.

"You need to have a come-to-Jesus meeting with them," said the CEO. (Of course he's a Northeastern Jew, but the ability to use such colorful Southern slang is part of what makes him folksy and successful.) "Sometimes," he added, "You just gotta punch people in the nose. They might punch you back, but at least you'll know where you stand."

Actually, the COO of the Power Trio had urged me to do the same thing—write down exactly what it was I needed. I think it's already a failure of communication that I've spent four months in somebody else's offices, and I have to write a memorandum to get my point across, but I'm good at writing stuff down, so I came up with a cover letter and four action points. I pled "I cannot succeed with you all being solely a source of passive capital—if that was all I needed, I would have stayed in New York, where my friends and contacts are."

Here's half of the letter, with some of their responses in italics:

> To: Power Trio
> From: Ali R.
> Re: Flipping Business Plan/Agenda
> Date: 24 January 2006
>
> I regret that we are not flipping already—but I think there were some critical misunderstandings about the nature of the venture...
>
> I feel like our meeting two weeks ago was really productive—since you've asked me to put down the things I need in writing, here are the top four:
>
> 1.   A speaking venue.
>   You've seen me in action at Inman Connect [a New York City real estate shebang where I moderated the last panel of the conference] and know I can motivate a crowd. (If I can

charm Realtors who are eager to catch flights home out of a three-day conference, imagine what I can do with motivated homeowners!)

Still, I haven't been able to set up anything on my own. I've tried the head of the library, pastors at a couple of local churches, reporters and publishers at a couple of local newspapers, the development person in the East Orange mayor's office, and [the city councilwoman who is a real estate agent in our office], and I've struck out all around, so I'll need your help setting up a seminar. Set me up with a place—which should be in a community setting, such as a church or a community center—and I've got the topics ready to go.

The response I got on this one: "That's long-term."

2. Time shadowing a more experienced agent.

"You seem to be struggling a lot with the basics," was a letter I got from a reader about my last column, and it's a comment I've gotten before. I need to watch an experienced agent do what they do—evaluate a house, talk to a homeowner, take a listing. I fully believe this kind of mentorship is the way to learn these skills. I've asked for this verbally before and got the answer, "Let's think who the right agent would be." Let me state now, in writing, that it's a big priority. And let me reiterate that I don't need to interfere with the senior agent's business in any way; for purposes of this learning exercise, I can be invisible.

This I got, right after I asked for it, and it was fabulous. [See the next chapter.] Half the real estate people I talk to say it was remarkably generous of a senior agent to share his mentoring and trade secrets; the other half say it's par for the course at their firms. I will say that later, when I went to work for DG Neary Realty in New York, I was only in the office for about 10 minutes before co-founder Gil Neary stuck me and another newbie agent in a cab and whisked us off to our first listing appointment.

3. A couple of starter listings.
    Traditionally, agents get these from floor time [basically, tak-
    ing a shift to answer the office phones and following up with
    whoever calls], which I've been told not to do. Some leads
    and listings are also parceled out by the firms themselves,
    and here I haven't gotten any, despite having a conversation
    with [firm president] and [listings manager].

    Your firm's Web technology is geared toward having listings,
    so once I have listings to pull consumers into my pages; it
    will enable me to spread the word to them about what I'm
    trying to do.

    [I knew that asking for this would be perceived as throw-
    ing down the gauntlet (and indeed, it was) but it's a basic
    question I have about real estate firms: *what happens to the
    leads that come in through the Web?* They've never ended up
    on my desk—and I've been led to believe, talking to agents
    in New York, that they never will. But it does seem that if a
    firm wanted to incubate or support an agent, that would be
    the mechanism. Real estate is a referral business, so why not
    seed the first few deals so that the referral network has a
    base from which to grow?]

    *The unofficial response I got on this one: Those choice Internet
    leads? 1) there aren't as many of them as the firms would
    have you think and 2) they're given as rewards to agents that
    are already producing. Milk is given to the teenagers, not the
    toddlers.*

4. Introductions to attorneys and insurance adjusters.
    I spent a lot of time at the Connect conference with a South
    Jersey flipper, who suggested I contact insurance adjusters.
    And [Power Trio CEO] has suggested estate attorneys. I'm
    happy to do direct mailings to those groups, but my experi-
    ence with builders is that cold letters don't work—and all my
    attorney and insurance connections are in New York, not here.
    Open the door for me with some of the Jersey people, and I'm
    sure I can sell them on the power of what we're trying to do.

[While I had some luck with direct mail straight to home-owners, I had already tried, as a step on this flipping path, to do cold letters to builders and it hadn't worked for me. I hear Coldwell Banker, a big national firm, has been starting to pursue the same strategy, and I wish them more success. But I thought, hey, the real estate community is small, and the people in this firm have been at it for decades; wouldn't it be nice if they introduced me to people who work in this industry? So I asked for it.]

What did they say? This was my Erin Brockovich moment. In the movie in my head, this is the scene that keeps repeating: I asked a guy who's been in the real estate business for 50 years to introduce me to local real estate attorneys, and he hands me a phone book. *A Yellow Pages. And I'm thinking, dear Lord, I left my* job *for this.*

Chapter 12

Shadowing Mr. Success

(A Jersey Broker's Tricks of the Trade)

So I'd been pushing and pushing for a number of things, and I was finally granted one: I would get to follow a senior broker-salesperson around.

The Power Trio picked someone who's truly one of the good guys, the kind of agent that has a smile (and a helpful tip) for every newbie. I'm going to show you the underside of his day, but I'm an ink-stained wretch with a conscience, so I'm going to change a detail or two to protect the anonymity of this agent: Let's call him Mr. Success.

First off, we agreed to meet in the office at 10:00. He actually showed at 10:30. (Have you ever met the real estate agent who could get any- where on time? I never have.) First thing, he mentions the newspaper. Our firm's press agent got a great placement in the local paper about one of our firm's properties, a restaurant that's for sale.

One eensy problem: The article in the paper indicates, wrongly, that the restaurant is closing.

So job one of the day is press management—trying to find and kill the reporter; trying to get the publisher to run a big screaming correction; reassuring the seller that our firm's in control of the restaurant sale despite the fact that customers, believing the restaurant to be closed, have stopped coming.

And of course, there's trying to find and kill the press agent; this, frankly, is a task I am familiar with. I am also ambivalent about what's going on; I know how easy it is to screw up a news report, and it may not have been his fault. On the other hand, the press agent is a "friend" of mine, somebody I had figured for a writing client, and I have not seen dollar one's worth of work out of him. In fact, he had actually introduced me to a client that was too cheap to hire me, so that proposal took two days of time I should have spent flipping. But hey, I'd landed my day with Mr. Success, so let's learn!

Mr. Success and I took a drive into Newark. He grew up in Newark and now sells property in the city, even though he's "made it" and moved to the 'burbs. He told me his aspiration is to stop selling so many multi-family investment properties and to start selling more single-family houses, which sets off a warning bell: Have I started at the wrong end of the business? I thought investment properties would be more fun and more lucrative—and Mr. Success is giving me the report from the trenches that they're harder.

We went to City Hall; in Newark, everything goes through City Hall. On the housing front, you can't sell a multifamily property without a certificate of occupancy, a C of O, saying that an inspector says the house is habitable and it's got X dwelling units. You can't in New York either, but the tricky thing about Newark is that C of Os don't last that long. So if you buy a house and decide to sell it a year later, your old C of O isn't good anymore, and you have to get an inspector out again.

The wait for an inspection, here in Boomtown, is a solid two months; of course, the inspector's probably going to find some defects that need to be cured. So you do that work, then you get the inspector out again, with another two-month delay.

Well, if real estate fans wanted to go that slowly they'd buy co-ops, not houses. As a shortcut, many Newark sellers take a hearing with the city and ask for a temporary C of O, so they can close sometime before Judgment Day.

Mr. Success tells me that some lenders (like Bank of America) won't take a temp C of O, so the game for a hard-working agent is to goose the inspection calendar, make sure pre-inspection work gets done, and to find a favorable lender.

That's a lot of value to a homeowner. On this transaction, it was imperative that Mr. Success move an inspection date up; his deal had to close by the end of the month or he was going to lose it. So we went in the bowels of City Hall, where a harassed clerk controls the housing of a quarter of a million people using the cutting-edge technology of a day planner and a bottle of Wite-Out.

I wish I were even half as charming as Mr. Success was that day. He somehow managed to establish that he and the clerk had both sent their kids to the same school—no mean feat because she was generally on three phone lines at once. Her calendar was booked solid, but she remembered some arcane clerky detail, moved things around like a sliding-tile puzzle where 15 pieces rejiggered, and bingo! She found the empty slot for an earlier inspection. (To those of you who are wondering about the character of your public servants, money did not change hands.)

Mr. S. then had to go to the bank, and he asked me to baby-sit his double-parked car. Okay, I thought. I can drive well enough to avoid getting carjacked. (Sure, it's a paranoid and racist and classist thought, but before you throw a stone, *you* go get a Betty Crocker haircut with some blonde highlights and then sit in a car in downtown Newark.) I did get approached, but it was by a 15-year-old who looked like a hooker, more likely beggar than carjacker. I didn't even roll down the window. I just did a dumb show: Look, lady, I'm not from here; I'm from Jupiter, which explains my hair. Whatever you want, it's not worth your time to convince me.

On the drive back to the office, Mr. Success is on the phone nearly as much as the clerk was, calling lawyers, updating them about the deal. I let him go for about 20 minutes, then between calls ask about the one thing I didn't understand—why try so hard to move an inspection date up by just two weeks? Who's in that kind of an all-fired hurry? "It's the buyer," he said. "She has to close by the end of the month. Has to."

"Can't she just extend her mortgage commitment by a couple of weeks?" I suggested.

"No, she's an investor," he said. When I didn't get it, he went on: "They ran her credit at the beginning of the month. Then she bought a house. If they run her credit again, they'll find *that* house, and they won't let her buy *this* house."

"Of course," I thought. Values are going up 31 percent a year here, and this really is the Wild Wild West. Mr. Success's obligation is to his seller, and he's getting a great price and providing a quick closing. He's being nice to me, and teaching me the ropes of the business. He's a good guy. So what if, when you think about it, the buyer's probably committing mortgage fraud? The banks are big enough to look after themselves (suddenly Bank of America seems a whole lot smarter).

I gave him the smile I'd just practiced, which I now think of as my Newark smile: Whatever you want to do, it's okay; it's not worth your time to convince me.

Chapter 13

The End of Jersey

(Admitting That "Flipping" Has Been a Total Failure)

I'VE SPENT FIVE months in New Jersey chasing my tail. I'm acutely aware that during that time, I could have written a book or learned French or picked up some marketable computer skills. But I had this dream that I could flip middle-class housing, and it was a pretty powerful dream: cash for distressed sellers, better housing for middle-class buyers, a decent living for me.

At the point where I'm ready to throw in the towel—and start down the path of getting my license in New York—there's one last swing I want to take: to speak at a sales meeting at my firm's South Orange office.

The office manager is incredibly eager to have me. He says that the office I'm based in is too upper-middle class (read: too rich and too white) and that the agents in his office will have the kind of rapidly gentrifying properties I'm looking for.

My first hint that something is very, very wrong is when the manager doesn't return my call to reconfirm the date. I finally wheedle out of the receptionist that he's actually been fired. One of my partners, the president of the firm, urges me to come in anyway.

Oh, c'mon dumbass, you my dear reader are thinking, *you know how this is gonna end.* Maybe I did, but I want to emphasize that I came from a corporate culture where I was rarely given an opening, so I am really used to finding some slim hope at all times, even if I have to invent it. Because if I don't brainwash myself that way, I can't get up in the morning. In order to function in a sexist world I have to believe that a ghost of a chance might exist.

So, expecting to find my ghost, I girded my loins (the modern way, by putting on pantyhose without any runs in them) and showed up to the sales meeting. It was packed; there were foil trays of chicken and a huge audience, probably 50 agents.

The agenda for the meeting ran to more than a dozen points, among them:

- Your firm's fantastic new technology;
- The latest co-op listings;
- What happened to the disappearing manager; and
- Me.

I gave the exact same presentation I'd given at my firm's home office.

Same emphasis lines, same jokes. Only this time, I bombed. I won a state speaking championship when I was in high school and I have bombed in a comedy club in downtown Manhattan; believe me, I know the difference.

The agents were restless, twitching their feet and shaking their heads at me. Once, when I was in my twenties, I read a humor piece at an open mike night. I was performing in a friendly space, with a warm, smoky, 420 vibe, and the piece had killed before. This time it didn't. Midway through, I heard one audience member say to another, "My god, she's terrible."

This felt like that.

I kept going because I am classy or stubborn or something, and then sat down. One of the agents in the back beckoned me over.

"The flip you're looking for, what made you think you could find a house like that?"

"I went over it with the Power Trio; we put together a business model; we expected to find six a year," I said.

"And how long have you been at this?"

"Several months."

"And how many have you found?"

"None."

"Didn't you wonder why? The reason is, if any of us found a house like that, we'd flip it ourselves. You're looking for something that is too good—and the people who own this company should know better."

Ow.

"I can't have any thinner a spread," I said, "because then I can't pay them."

"Your partners? What do you need them for? To get you a mortgage? You find a house this good, any banker in the world will write you a mortgage," said the agent. "The partners would just be trying to stick a finger in your cookie jar. Except that they didn't tell you it's impossible in the first place. They're just trying to pimp you out. If you get lucky, they make money, and it doesn't hurt *them* if you fail. They're just trying to pimp you out."

My chest hurt, very badly. I thanked that agent and went over to the next agent, who told me the same thing—the kind of house I wanted to flip would be a winning lottery ticket, and who wouldn't pick it up? And then a third time, the same remarks, from a nice grandmotherly woman this time.

After making my excuses to my partners, I left the office, collapsing into sobs. I cried for three hours.

First, I wandered blindly for a few moments. In suburban Jersey, wandering blindly on foot at night, with no Springsteen soundtrack, isn't a beautiful thing. Then I got on a train home, convulsing with tears; the other passengers kept looking at me sideways, sympathetically, trying to figure out who died.

I was so upset that I called my mother, who isn't the right person to call when you've just fucked up a career, not because she doesn't have sympathy but because she's a Southern judge, and her tolerance for stupidity is small. I got home and had a fight with my husband for somehow not understanding me, and cried some more. Poor me. Poor, poor, pitiful me. I felt conned. All the risks I had taken, and the tens of thousands of dollars I had blown through, and for what? A dream that didn't exist—a mirage. And I had learned that it didn't exist because my firm's own agents had told me.

Couldn't somebody have pointed this out five months ago?

PART II

New York

Chapter 14

Class, Again

*(A Harvard-Educated Real Estate Agent Learns
about UFOs)*

AFTER A LOT of soul-searching, I decided to take my license in New
York. To say that I was plagued with doubt would have been an under-
statement. I have sold my stock (the savings from 17 years of hard work),
blown the wedding money, and run through most of the second mortgage on the beach house. I have, for the first time in my life, a five-figure
MasterCard debt that won't go away. In response to the money crunch,
my darling husband, who was already working a ten-to-seven regular job,
started taking freelance work, staying up until midnight or one some
nights just to get some extra income in.

I'd sent out queries about editorial jobs, and threw my hat in the ring
for the editorship of the *Village Voice* (the job ended up going to a Washington, DC, editor who gave one newsroom talk and left a mere two weeks
later) and *Haute Living* (whose publisher offered me $40 an hour, less than
my last job). I hadn't tapped my 401(k) yet, but I was eyeing it. So what
was I thinking, starting over in New York? In five months, I hadn't generated any real estate activity whatsoever—so now I'm going to throw good
money after bad?

The positive case, the one I talked myself into, is that straight selling would probably be easier than flipping because some of the properties start out in good shape in the first place. In a sense, I already knew the New York City (especially Manhattan) inventory—I'd written about it for two years. But most importantly, if I was going to have to rely on my "warm market" (a phrase I've always translated as "the kindness of my friends"), it would have to be in New York.

Compared to Jersey, where the training was rigorous, the New York classes turn out to be a joke. Salesperson licensure comes after 45 hours, not 75. The classes themselves are jammed, with newcomers inhaling to try to squeeze into non-aisles between broken desks. The instructors avoid answering tough questions (such as "do I need to be at one of the big firms to have good co-op comps, or will the smaller shared listings services have them?"). The low point is when one particularly long-winded instructor, whose diatribe against rent control we've already been forced to endure, tells us that UFOs are real because his daughter saw one.

And here I am arguing that there's professionalism in my industry.

On the other hand, there are some high points. Some of the instructors make us role play, which does zero for our exam skills but is incredibly helpful in terms of career prep. One instructor in particular, Bill Plunkett, makes sure we can talk to a customer about a listing, weed out browsers from buyers, and spot traps where we'd be tempted to practice law.

In general, though, the class's fluidity hurts us. In Jersey, we were there at the same time every day: Steve (ended up at Coldwell Banker) third desk back on the right, Sue (ended up at Burgdorff ERA) first desk on the left. Here, I try to meet my fellow students—I know they'll be an asset when they're at a big firm like Elliman and I'm wherever—but it's tough to network with people I see in only a single three-hour session. I feel like I'm in a bar picking up strangers, most of whom don't know that they're there to be picked up.

I zero in on one woman, basically because she's the wealthiest woman in class. (Money can't buy happiness, but it can buy some kick-ass shoes.) She looks porcelain and untouchable, like a 50-year-old version of Selma Blair. I go up and talk to her, which I gather people just don't do. It turns out she has run a major nonprofit, which she's surprised I've heard of. And then she's not exactly flattered, more like a little freaked, when she tells me which brokerage firm she's interviewing with and I offer to drop a word to the CEO.

I actually do send an enthusiastic e-mail to the head of that firm, displaying a degree of follow-through that is somewhat uncharacteristic of me. I don't often make good on my good impulses; I'm more often Our Lady of the Intended Thank-You Note. But I figure this one's for karma.

Chapter 15

Taking a Listing

(Things Every Smart Seller Should Know)

"SO YOU GUYS wanna come take a listing?"

I couldn't believe it. It was my second day on the job in New York, and my sponsoring broker wanted me to go along as he took a listing? I hung out in Jersey for months and never managed to glom on to anyone who was doing that.

When I pointed that out to him, his attitude was, "Well, how else are you going to learn?" So I jumped into the cab.

There were actually four of us—but let me back up. On deciding I was going to work in New York, my next question was, *where?*

I worked the connections I had made at the *New York Post* when I covered real estate, and talked to executives at many different brokerage houses. It turns out there were two kinds of brokerage houses: big houses that knew about my column and didn't want me to write about them, and big houses that didn't want me to take listings at 5 percent.

For those of you who don't know New York City, let me say that the commission debate that has hit the rest of the country is raging here. Some listings go through at five (one senior agent at one of the top five

SIX THINGS EVERY SMART SELLER SHOULD KNOW

1.   **Interview at least three agents.** Comparison gives you the easiest way to notice where an agent is weak or leaving something out.
2.   **What should you ask?** Judging from listing pitches, sellers ask how they can get a million dollars for a cramped home without redoing the bathroom. Wait, I'm kidding, don't ask that. But do ask at what price the agents would list your home (and why); what price they'd expect to get (and when); and what Plan A they have in place to get there and what Plan B looks like. Ask what average days on market are for your type of listing, and what comparable sales prices are. *Nota bene:* Anybody who says they can substantially beat the comps is probably lying.
3.   **Hire the person you're comfortable doing business with— not necessarily the one you like best.** This is a tough piece of advice for me to give, because we agents cultivate likeability, and it's one of my strong suits. But selling a home requires

firms told me that 20 percent of their listings did), but there's a lot of denial. One very popular theme is "keeping up appearances." This means a firm will take a listing at 5 percent but instead of offering a straight one-half of that (what we call the *co-broke*) to the agent who brings in the buyer, they will offer the co-broke at three. The outside world assumes that the listing broker is getting double the co-broke, or 6 percent, when in reality, they're just getting their margins squeezed—which certainly sounds like bad business, long-term. Not that I always wanna go out at five, but hey, flexibility is nice.

So I ended up working for the broker who sold me my very first apartment. Gil Neary has the fine bones and long hair of a Renaissance prince, but he doesn't have any of the aloofness that usually goes with that more than just charm, and you want the total package: a strategic plan, access to buyers, attention to detail, willingness to work.

4. **Hire someone you think is honest, or at least acceptably dishonest.** I once went on a listing pitch and asked the seller about my competition, and she said, "Well, Bob told me my apartment was worth $50,000 more than you did, and I'm pretty sure he's lying, but he was so good at it I thought he might be able to convince somebody else." Point taken, but isn't that like hiring a dishonest lawyer? He'll nominally represent you, but if he's that good at lying, where's he screwing you?

5. **Know what your escape routes are.** Make sure the listing contract has an acceptable time limit, and know under what circumstances you can break it.

6. **Tell your agent what you expect of her—and find out what she expects on your side.** If she wants access to the house, access to your friends' e-mail addresses, or a complete kitchen makeover, you need to know that in advance.

appearance. Gil's one of those people who's successful in real estate because he's tremendously social—he makes hundreds of friends, and then sells apartments to all of them. His schtick is to make sure everyone is settled in just the right home, and then to watch that they stay happy in it. He's an old-fashioned ward boss who knows about countertops.

Gil's long list of friends and clients includes me, and in my case it's been repeat business: Gil sold me my first studio, and then handled the sale when I moved up to something bigger. When I bought my first condo, I'd found it through an ad in the paper, but I had liked him enough to bring him in as my broker. I thought he'd be a pretty good boss, but I had no idea how good.

At the listing presentation, he let Michael, the agent whose deal it was, do most of the talking, stepping in as the voice of authority only when needed. Then afterward, he explained to me and another newbie why he'd said what he'd said.

Have you ever been at a corporate meeting where a manager stopped to explain to you why he said what he said? Me neither. But the patterning turned out to be helpful when I took my very own FIRST LISTING one week later. Yes! Me, the failure! Spring had sprung, and I had real estate to sell!

Of course I had hoped this was coming, since Persephone, one of my old friends, had said that she would be happy to list her apartment with me. That's trust: giving your listing to someone you went to college with, knowing full well that she is inexperienced *and* demoralized.

I know P. did it partly as a gift; here, let me jump-start your business. Still, so many people have told me shiny happy things over the past year, and they haven't always turned out to be true.

This, however, did. And now I had a mission: to sell the most beautiful $519K-one-bedroom I'd ever seen in my life.

Chapter 16

Staging the Bohemian Apartment

(Where to Put the Bong before the Open House)

BORED WITH YOUR standard exercise routine? Try photographing a small apartment.

I was excited to have my first listing, and for starters I did what I would tell any seller to do: booked a professional real estate photographer. I wasn't taking the actual pictures, but I still showed up to do the *staging* (the current real estate buzzword for making a place salesworthy: a combination of cleaning, interior decorating, and out-and-out fluffing).

I knew roughly what the one-bedroom I had listed looked like—it was owned by my friend P. and I had been in it numerous times; in fact, I'd made her buy it. Still, she'd rented it out for months, and when I got in to see it, I was a bit dismayed to see the tenant had left both the Swiffer and the vacuum cleaner sitting in the entryway. It's hard for buyers to swallow the claim of "great closet space" if the vacuum cleaner is just hanging out in all the photos, so the next hour was a game of moving the vacuum cleaner to the living room so the foyer could be photographed; moving the dirty dishes into the foyer so the kitchen could be photographed; moving the ashtrays into the bedroom so the living room could be photographed; and moving the laundry and guitars into the living room so the bedroom could be photographed.

STAGING THE BOHEMIAN APARTMENT

First, throw out or store one-third of what you own, and put some new white towels in the bathroom. (If that seems too hard, go buy a copy of *Staging for Dummies*.) Then, you'll want to apply these tips, some of which have already appeared in my column in the *New York Blade*.

1. **Hide any evidence that you have fun.** This means bongs, this means ashtrays, this means videogames, this means porn. (When the listing above finally closed, the buyer was puzzled by the presence of duct tape on the edge of the windows; I thought, "um, to keep the smoke from leaking out?") Just remember that not everyone has the same taste, and too much visual information is going to turn off straight-laced buyers with kids.

2. **Candles are for light only.** This is the leading instance of where preciousness can go too far: You spend hours to hit the right mind-body-spirit balance of sandalwood, rosemary and ylang-ylang, and your potential buyer turns out to be allergic. While you're at it, pay attention to how your whole home smells: carpets should be freshly clean, cat litter should be newly changed, drains should have baking soda dumped into them. You want to go for an absence of smells, rather than a perfumy quality, though the old real estate agent's standby of baking cookies during an open house never hurt anybody.

Thankfully, the bathroom was pretty okay.

Oh, the tenant had tried; his laundry was neatly piled, and the thing that looked like a bong (but that I'm *sure* was an ironic piece of sculpture) was thoughtfully shoved into the kitchen cabinet. But I couldn't get over the mess! I called Gil, the King of Tact, who paused for a moment and said, "Well, he's not a decorator."

P. had asked me what she should do to get her asking price—glaze the tub? Redo the plasterwork? Now, after an hour in the apartment, I had the answer. "Rent your tenant a storage space, so that his suitcases don't

If you think you're too desensitized to the way your place smells, have a friend walk through and "sniff test" for you.

3. **If you go over the top, go way *way* over.** When I advise sellers, it's all about "depersonalization"—I tell them to take out the family photos and kids' soccer trophies and other specific knickknacks that will make it hard for a buyer to picture themselves in that home. But if you've got the Armani Casa gene, and you've up and imported carved doors from Italy to fulfill your medieval fantasy, you're in too deep already; go ahead and leave a silver chalice out on the mantelpiece.

   The one corollary to this rule is that collections must breathe: buyers want to see luxurious empty space around each piece. If you're selling, put half your Fiestaware in storage now.

4. **Don't make your house seem too perfect to live in.** I'm not saying you should leave your Kleenex boxes out, but you don't want to give off the "high-design hotel" vibe either. Try for a homey contrasting touch, like a fruit bowl in a Neutra-inspired modern space. House-hunting is thirsty work, too, so put out a pitcher of lemonade in the summer or a jug of cider in the winter.

take up the front closet; then there'd be a place to put the vacuum cleaner and the Swiffer."

Despite the clutter, I made three appointments to show the place that next week. It was relatively cheap for Manhattan—i.e., under $550K—and agents had been eagerly calling about it. I wanted to make it as available as possible; I knew from my own experience trying to place renters how frustrating it was to work with a place you couldn't see.

The day of the first showings, I felt pretty ready to go. I finished up some writing in the morning, and although I had a terrible cold, I could just manage to hold my head up without looking like I was suffering from a grisly hangover. My watch matched my blouse, and I left myself just enough time to swing by the office and see if my business cards had come in so that I had something to hand out.

Hand out ... omigod, sell sheets! Don't apartments usually come with sell sheets? Three nice customers are going to walk in the door, see the premises, and I'm going to hand them ... what? I have no collateral material!

For heaven's sake, I thought, I'm a writer; all I do is produce printed crap all day long, and now I don't have any.

I tore out of the house, hair flying, deciding that I could still make my first appointment if I skipped going to the office. If I could somehow whip up a sell sheet I'd be okay; I could explain away the absence of business cards by telling customers that my contact information was on the sheet. I gambled against going to the Kinko's near me, betting I could find one nearer the listed apartment. I put on my makeup while I was being jostled on the subway (not for nothing have I lived in New York for two decades) and I got to the place with half an hour to spare.

Apparently, my lecture to the tenant about cleanliness and godliness had sunk in somewhat. I still had to hide a few pairs of shoes, but the clothes I had folded and put in the closet a few days ago were still neat, and the dishes were done. I picked a living room corner to stash the vacuum cleaner in, just so it wasn't the first thing a buyer would see, and headed out to the street with 15 minutes to go.

Across the street from the apartment was the kind of hipster café where kids form bands, and I noticed with delight it had Internet access, and printers! God loves me. (The blessings of health and family may not have opened my eyes to that fact, but finding an Internet café in the desert sure did.)

I popped open a Word document and wrote the address and price of my listing at the top; my three strongest selling points (e.g., pet-friendly building!) next, and then, zoom, I pulled a floor plan off my Webmail, and stuck my name and phone number at the bottom.

I noticed that the photos I had taken earlier were actually on the server now, but resizing them on the fly just seemed way too complicated, so I went with just the floor plan. The resulting sell sheet was black-and-white, but otherwise not bad.

And I was only five minutes late when I crossed back to the lobby to meet the first customers of the day.

Chapter 17

Why Cheap Rentals Suck

(Meditations on Why Big-City Apartments Are Such a Rip-Off)

I HAVE NO clients.

Okay, that's not true, I have one listing to sell, but I have no other seller or buyer clients. There are a number of ways to attack this problem, and I have been trying them all. I've been spending most of my time attempting a classic Manhattan strategy: to start with renters.

Renters, the theory goes, grow up to be buyers—and then sellers. The best renters, of course, are budding doctors and lawyers; find a law student a rental today, and in three years, the theory goes, you sell them a million-dollar condo.

The only problem with this theory is that it doesn't work. Oh sure, a happy renter might turn into a happy buyer, down the road; but it's next to impossible, in this market, to create a happy renter.

It isn't for lack of product: three of every four households in Manhattan rent. The vacancy rate, however, is a swooningly low 4 percent. And the co-brokering system, which works pretty well when you're selling and the commission pie is big, suddenly founders when there's only a tartlet to share.

First, a quick look in the real estate database many New York City brokers use: there are 100 apartments priced under $2,000 a month in the downtown (below 34th Street) area. If I need to find a client a starter apartment, a 1-in-100 shot ought to be enough.

But unlike sales listings, rental listings come without floor plans and usually without photos. The database is a furniture store where all the sofas are shrouded; even in a world of cell-phone cameras, I can't tell what the hell the apartments are going to look like. Some of the listings do come with photos of the *exteriors* of their buildings, but I think that's the equivalent of selling me fried chicken by showing me the feathers.

I bumble through the listings, discarding the old (has that unit really been on the market for 147 weeks?) and the too-obviously small (if they say it's 300 square feet, what is it really?). Then I pick a handful that sound nice and start making phone calls.

"Hi, I'm an agent calling for a client" is not what these people want to hear. Many of them tell me flat out they won't co-broke, figuring that I have better things to do than to tattle on them individually to the real estate board—sadly, they're usually right. A search of Craigslist is no better; I'd say at least half of the value-priced apartments, if they ever existed in the first place, disappear when brokers hear I'm a pro.

One possibility is to send my poor little client directly to a rental agency, where the wolves will feast on her themselves. This may get her access to apartments she couldn't see without me, but it may not: For the client, it's the luck of the draw, and it does nothing to improve my client relations.

The other option is to show the client co-brokered apartments, but then—yes, this is legal—the fee goes up. Most listing brokers will charge a renter 12 percent of a year's rent: at $2,000, that's $2,880, which is a pretty significant chunk of change. To bring me in, they'll jack the fee up to 15 percent to make room for the co-broke.

Trying desperately to justify my value, I at least go the personal-shopper route to weed out the dreck. And there is dreck: a "loft" turns out to

THE GREATEST RENTAL SEARCH TIP EVER

This comes from an actual renter, Dan Cea, who was interviewed by Suzanne Markert in the January 4, 2004, edition of the *New York Post.* Take a heavy book—a Tom Wolfe hardback, say, or a cookbook—with you on your apartment search. If you find something you like, "accidentally" drop it. *Voilà!* You have just flushed out all the barking dogs and crying babies in the building.

be a studio, 17 feet square, with the kitchen in a corner (they could have written that in the listing, but who would come?) and a "two-bedroom" turns out to be a Habitrail with slightly higher ceilings and worse closets. My new cell phone is a godsend here, because I can at least aim the camera at a living room and send an image to my client in real time.

Even if I find something decent, I have to go back to my client, who, remember, I am trying to cultivate as a source of future income, and explain that I have just found her a great apartment that she probably could have pulled off of Craigslist, but because of my expertise, and the day I saved her from looking at junk, she gets to pay me an additional $720. This is a newly minted lawyer with $100,000 worth of loans on her back, and instead of debt-servicing them for a month or buying a big new TV, she gets to pay me $100 an hour for saving her the trouble of looking at *six* lousy apartments.

Even car salesmen, as maligned as they are, don't always make the consumer's first point of contact with their industry the most expensive and worst experience the consumer is going to have. Only real estate agents do that. No wonder people think we're schmucks.

Chapter 18

Breaking into a Suburban House

(That I Just Happened to Own)

IT TAKES LESS than 15 minutes to break into an average suburban house; I know because I did it a couple of weeks ago. The house in question was my own, a two-family property on Long Island's South Shore. It's the first and only house I've ever owned, and boy, it's been nothing but trouble.

The break-in first: My contractors were due out, and I had hopped a train from the city to meet them, but of course I forgot to grab the correct set of keys. Rescheduling these guys would take two weeks at least, so instead of hauling back to the city, I popped out a basement window instead. To get inside, I had to jump down six feet, and I'm no Lucy Liu, so it looked like 60; I finally poked a broomstick down into the basement to pull the dehumidifier over for a landing pad.

I'm a little ashamed to say that none of my neighbors—at least one of whom was out in her yard—questioned why someone in a nice suburban area was clumsily wriggling into a basement in broad daylight. (Note to potential thieves: there's nothing in the house but some broken Pier

One furniture and some old college textbooks; don't bother.) Maybe my neighbors were just enjoying the fact that I had to take out two window panes to get my hips through.

The point, I guess, is that half-million-dollar suburban houses aren't all that secure. "Safe as houses"—what does that mean? Which brings us to the trouble: I bought this house five years earlier, after an awful breakup, thinking I just needed to get away—from the city, from the wreck of my engagement. I was so lost; the only thing I could think was that it would be fun to have sand squish between my toes.

No one warned me that it would stick in my craw as well. In the five years since I bought the house, when it had a decent inspection, I've replaced the roof ($5,700 plus the cost of having interior work to repair water damage), the hot water heater ($650 plus the cardio-blast experience of receiving a $900 water bill) and the garage door (who knew they cost $900?). I still haven't redone the driveway, which has more deep cracks and lines than a Shar-Pei, because I can't bear to spend the $5,000.

Also, here's a lament familiar to American homeowners, my property taxes have doubled—in five years! I guess I should have known never to move to an area that's been famous for corruption for decades.

Then there was the bad tenant; let's call him Rob, because that's his name, and he still owes me money. Rob started off fine, then fell behind on his rent, forcing me to evict him, which was costly. Then he left for Vegas, leaving me holding all of his stuff.

Which, legally, you can't just throw out on the lawn. So his stuff (really broken Pier One furniture and old dog toys) was sitting in my basement, which flooded and turned into Mold City. Did you know it costs $5,000 to rip out a basement down to the studs so the mold remediation guys can do their thing? I'm sadder but wiser now.

$5,700, $650, $900, $900, $5,000 ... plus the nail-biting tax bills.

The result, of course, is that I love the house in a way I'll never love my city apartment. Am I a masochist? Maybe, but there's something more:

TIPS FOR GETTING A GOOD LONG-TERM RETURN ON A HOUSE

1. Try to buy only when you have a time frame of five years or more; that way, if there's a short-term downturn in the market, you can ride it out.
2. Imagine who your future buyer would be and make sure that dovetails with trends in your area. For example, if school enrollment is declining, who's going to be the future buyer for your four-bedroom house?
3. Don't buy an outlier: if your neighborhood is full of Victorians, it's probably risky to buy the one contemporary on the block.
4. Don't rush! You'll either buy the wrong house or pay too much for the right one, because you won't feel you have the leisure to negotiate. Getting a short-term rental and moving all your furniture twice might cost you $10,000; rushing to buy too quickly certainly will.
5. Buy the worst house on the best block, not the best house on the worst block. It's an old real estate saw, but it's true; stretch financially, if you have to, to get into a good neighborhood, and your house will benefit from being in the company of more expensive homes.

I feel centered in it. Its pipes feel like my veins—possibly because they've been directly transplanted from me through my wallet.

My house's financial troubles were top-of-mind because of where I was in my career—hawking a half-a-million dollar listing, and thus meeting a lot of first-time buyers. Here's what they're facing: city prices are running hot at an average of $1,000 a square foot.

To explain how ridiculously expensive this is, let me quote writer David Abramowicz: He suggested that you dump a bag of $100 bills out onto the floor of the apartment, and spread them around. If you can still see the floor, you haven't got enough money for the apartment.

Another way to think about it is that for your $500K you're only getting a one-bedroom. Why pay that? Because houses seem so scary. Just to keep up with an old house in the 'burbs requires an every-third-Saturday willingness to deal with contractors. And let's go back to the money: my actual yearly expenses (taxes, heat, repairs, insurance) are $20,000, plus mortgage interest of another $15,000. A hundred dollars a day, just for heat and entropy! And this is on the starter plan, where I'm a landlady and don't even get to live in the whole house.

The balm, for me as it has been for everybody, has been rising home values. I interviewed Ben Bernanke for *The Daily Deal* when he was one of the governors of the Federal Reserve, not yet chairman, and he said, "The debt increases we've seen have been mortgage debt, a smart kind of debt for consumers to have, and most of it has been taken on by people who are not terribly leveraged."

That was in 2003, and those consumers have only been helped by a generally booming market. The costs are scary, but the equity is soothing—I guess that's why we're all Zillow freaks, constantly checking the valuation site (*www.zillow.com*) to see what our homes are worth. Me, I bought for $400K, and I believe my hanging in and re-roofing could generate $600K, despite five years' worth of wear and tear on the kitchens and bathrooms. That's way better than my supposedly "safe" 401(k) has been doing in the stock market. It means I've been making capital gains of $110 a day, just for flipping burgers on the grill and putting up with the vagaries of some contractors. Like I tell first-time buyers, what else are you going to do with your time?

Chapter 19

Testing, Testing

(Do I Have the Personality of a Successful Agent?)

As a rookie who had yet to connect with my first pitch, I was reading everything: *Realtor* magazine; *The Wall Street Journal;* the Craigslist housing forum; and spam about how to "sell better faster." So, of course, when it came across my radar, I eagerly read Bernice Ross's three-part series on agent success. For those of you who missed it, RealEstateCoach. com (which is her site) partnered with iSucceed.com and the Real Estate Simulator (*www.realestatesimulator.com*) to find the correlates of success for rookie agents. This is the Web, not the *New England Journal of Medicine,* so I take what I read with a grain of salt, but I'm encouraged by the findings that rookie success is not about age or about gender.

What they did find correlated was performance on the Real Estate Simulator and a couple of personality tests. I flipped through the Real Estate Simulator demo, and it looked, to me, like stuff that could be taught—you're given a situation where you have your foot in the door, and you get video of a recalcitrant homeowner, and you're supposed to select what to say to him. They had us do simulations at the firm in Jersey and it seems like some of what gets trained into you is phrases ("top dollar" when you're speaking to sellers, for example). It also seems like some of what gets trained into you is your own comfort with the process, so you learn to talk to a homeowner in a poised way, like it's something you do every day. Maybe there's some value to learning to say the phrase "top dollar" without rolling your eyes at the plasticity of it.

Anyway, I skipped that part and went straight for the personality tests. I had never seen the DISC, a personality profiler that measures you on four scales: Dominance, Influence, Steadiness, and Conscientiousness. Unlike Myers-Briggs, a personality profile test that I was familiar with, it doesn't generate suggested job choices, like teacher or architect. Instead it tells you about your work style: are you critical, do you take risks? I couldn't find a DISC book in Barnes & Noble, but the test is available all over the Web, with insta-scoring. So I paid $27 for a 28-question test and downloadable results assessment from *www.corexcel.com*.

Now I could not have gotten into Harvard without being a pretty good test-taker, and getting two real estate licenses brought me back up to speed, so I wasn't that worried about one more exam, although I did arm myself with a cup of tea and a box of shortbread.

Four choices were available for each test question, and you were supposed to pick which described you "most" at work, and which described you "least" at work. For example, which of the following words describes you most at work: a) argumentative; b) systematic; c) cooperative; or d) light-hearted? Which describes you least?

Some of the words looked pretty close together: I had a little trouble deciding whether I was *precise* or *direct*. (I went with *direct*.) And what the hell kind of person is going to call herself captivating?

Even worrying over these details, and munching on my cookies, the whole test, with scoring, took only about 10 minutes. And then I had my personality result: I'm an asshole.

Actually, a supreme asshole. The Dominance scale, or D-scale, has 28 questions, and I scored a 27 on it. This means I fit the Developer profile:

I'm daring and demanding, the makings of a great leader, if anyone else could stand to be in the same room with me. (*Egocentric* and *domineering* were the more negative words used on this scale; I called my sister, who's a psychologist, and she said, "Well, I don't know anything about the validity of this test, but on the face of it …")

Now the good news: according to Ross's article, a high D-score is one of the predictors of rookie agent success (so that's where Realtors' image problems come from). Other factors include a high Influence score—successful agents are highly persuasive, sociable people, probably the same people who call themselves captivating—and a willingness to work at least 35 hours per week. Having a financial motivation rather than an aesthetic or intellectual one (in other words, being money-grubbing) doesn't hurt either.

So I'm heartened that I've got the right stuff, even if the ingredients are those for a CEO from hell. It sounds like the things that would help me most would be a little bit of structure (so I don't go winging off into outer space on the pursuit of the next great idea) and to push up my influence by getting out there and contacting and entertaining people. This is stuff I think I already knew—for example, I've begun to have a nearly fanatical devotion to making lists—but it helps me plan for the future to have it all written down in black-and-white. I'm precise, I mean direct, that way.

Chapter 20

Clients, 90210

(Young Buyers and How to Be One)

ARMED WITH THE result of my personality test, I am trying to be more outgoing and friendly. At least showing P.'s apartment is starting to attract other potential clients. I hold my open houses, and I fasten like a tick to everyone who walks in the door or even calls, and that's how I got these clients I refer to in my head as "Buyers, 90210." The handle came about because of their relative youth (they're recent college graduates who want to be roommates) and because one of them works for a record company. I don't think these clients are naïve Brandons by any means—they both grew up in the city—but there is also a certain fresh-faced appeal about them that makes me want to mom them a little. I regard their desire for a cheap two-bedroom not as an impossibility, but as a challenge.

One possibility is to sell them a one-bedroom they could subdivide, but in the world of New-York-City-is-not-like-anywhere-else, this strategy would have to get past a co-op board. It has crossed my mind to let a Greenwich Village board hypothesize its own relationship between two young male buyers, but it would be so much easier for everyone to sell them an actual two-bedroom. So I was thrilled when I found one.

They were not convinced; the area was the Lower East Side, one that's been touted for years as up-and-coming, but on the fringes of the East Village, the neighborhood where they actually wanted to be. Still, I fell in love with the floor plan, and I pushed it. *Foolish, foolish girl.*

I figured out my mistake when I went to a midday open house at the prospective apartment, determined to pick up more collateral material to help me make my case, and found the neighborhood skanky. The listing was near a school (which I don't like categorically on the grounds that kids can be thugs without penalty) and, as I crossed the playground area, I caught three teenagers eyeing my engagement ring. If I feel menaced in the afternoon, I wondered, what's it going to be like at night?

The apartment itself was perfect, and by that I mean improved to within an inch of its life: dishwasher, washer/dryer, cute little balcony. Yet all that kept going through my head was "they can't live here, they can't live here." I asked the listing agent about the neighborhood, and he said, "Well, the presence of the school is absolutely great! Whenever there's a school, there's extra police presence." Great. I could just see this on Craigslist: "2-BR, 1-BA, extra police presence!!"

I headed off to another appointment, first walking half a mile to get to an Internet café and drop my buyers a note. "It would be racist and classist to say 'you can't live here,'" I thought. I remembered that agents can't say much about demographics (it's too easy to violate fair housing laws), that my obligations were to the seller, not the buyers, and that I almost hadn't seen my first apartment in Manhattan on the grounds that the agent refused to show it to me because that the fringe of Chelsea was not then suitable for a single female.

So I wrote a note telling the buyers I didn't think it was "a fit." I thought about using "edgy" or "block-by-block," but finally decided to call the neighborhood "too dingy." (I can almost hear my friend Lockhart Steele howling that I am dissing his beloved Lower East Side. But remember, dear readers, this word choice is coming from somebody who has walked through a Newark crack house.)

I wondered if my young clients thought I was a moron for not having known that my inventory was in an unacceptable neighborhood in the first place. But I just kept picturing walking their parents down the block. What, precisely, are my ethical obligations to the seller versus my obligations to the parents to keep their kids from getting mugged? Maybe, I thought, the buyers will appreciate the honesty. So imagine how happy I was to see this in my in-box later that day: "Went down there at 6. Had the same feelings as you."

What makes young buyers tick? Two professors, François Ortalo-Magné of the University of Wisconsin-Madison and Sven Rady of the University of Munich, have created a life-cycle model of the housing market. If I can grossly oversimplfy years of painstaking research, because I didn't actually talk to them, what the professors came out with is this: People buy depending on where they are in the life cycle. Young people buy starter homes, and later, when their income grows and they (hopefully) make capital gains, they trade up to new homes.

Certainly demographers can demonstrate that older people have higher rates of homeownership than younger people: Ogilvy & Mather says that nearly 80 percent of the baby boomers own homes, while only two-thirds of Gen Xers and less than half the so-called millenials do. What's striking about the Ortalo-Magné/Rady model of the world is that prices of homes are largely driven, not by the entire pool of buyers, but by the starter buyers. How much money the newbies make and how liberal lenders are with them establishes what kind of down payment they can raise; when they can make a down payment on a starter home, they buy it.

How does this square with our anecdotal reports that prices for starter homes are out of sight? Well, first-timers are using today's liberal credit to pile on plenty of debt. In 1999, according to the National Association of Realtors (NAR) Profile of Home Buyers and Sellers, the average starter buyer put $5,000 down on a $104K home; six years later, that down payment on a $150K home had fallen to just 2 percent. The 2005 NAR profile reports that 43 percent of first-timers are buying *with no money down whatsoever.* Pass the crack!

Manhattan is a little bit of a different market, because co-ops are going to call for 20 percent down, and most condos 10 percent (yes, Virginia, you can buy certain condos for only 5 percent down; call me).

Has the fact that starter buyers still have to put in a significant down payment restrained starter prices? Unfortunately, no. What it has meant is that you need more than one income. Let me quote Stuart Elliott, the editor of *The Real Deal,* from 2004, "Unless you have a comfy job on Wall Street, are heir to a mining and smelting fortune, or are a bank robber, coming up with the money to join the ranks of Manhattan homeowners can seem like an impossible task."

In the two years since Elliott wrote those words, entry-level prices have bumped up from being in the $200Ks to being in the high $300Ks. So what first-time buyers in Manhattan are doing (besides weeping) is relying harder on two incomes. Sometimes it's Mom and Dad's—I can tell you that "guarantors OK" is even better ad copy than "granite kitchen." Sometimes it's a couple, gay or straight, buying a studio (so the storage in the basement goes like hotcakes).

In some neighborhoods, the imbalance between starter home prices and incomes is so pronounced that current residents can't afford to buy there. I remember being on a panel with a couple of real estate agents and a couple of lenders at the Harlem Home Fair. The room was packed, and the attendees were very interested in learning how to buy their first apartments. My co-panelists offered advice on how to present yourself as an applicant and how to improve your credit score; I told the audience to go look in the South Bronx. The incomes of the people I was talking to were no match for the dizzying spiral of prices; they needed apartments that cost $100K, and they weren't going to find them locally in Harlem.

The whole Harlem situation has produced a pretty interesting loop-

RULES OF THUMB FOR YOUNG BUYERS

- ꝺ Hoard 10 percent of your nest egg for closing and moving costs.
- ꝺ Plan for a three-month period of illness or unemployment.
- ꝺ Set up an exit timetable, even if you don't end up following it.
- ꝺ Prenup if you're an unmarried couple or otherwise co-buying.
- ꝺ Expect to spend two years repairing and furnishing before you're "done."

hole in the luxury condo market. Many of the new condos have units set aside for current Harlem residents, who of course can't afford them even at "preferential" prices. (The median household income in Central Harlem, according to data provider OnBoard LLC, is less than $26,000 a year.) So if you want a deal on a Harlem condo, go live in the area for a year, establish yourself as a resident of Community Board 10, and then enter the lottery for locals. I'm not guaranteeing you a win, but I sure am shortening your odds.

As bad as it is in New York, it's worse in San Francisco. (Thanks to my Bay Area friend Stephanie Losee for pointing this out, and doing a nice piece for the *New York Post* with this theme: check out her magnificence at *www.stephanielosee.com.*) In Frisco, which faces the similar problem of very limited prime city land being fought over by people with seemingly unlimited incomes, buyers join together to purchase buildings, and then wait to win the city lottery so they can convert to condos. I'm not kidding; in this form of ownership, called *tenancy in common* (TIC), people who aren't necessarily related to each other act as co-borrowers for a single building loan. *Hey, you seem nice, wanna share a mortgage?*

Now you may be shaking your head knowingly, and going, oh, a co-op. But TICs can be much riskier. For one thing, TICs tend to be small, so instead of sharing the risks of a 100-unit building, you're sharing the risks of a four-unit Victorian house. In a co-op of 100 owners, a default is a drag; in a TIC of four, it's a disaster. And because you can't always get your own little fractional slice-of-heaven loan, you're stuck in lockstep with your co-borrowers if you want to, say, refinance. Housing does, indeed, make strange bedfellows.

Chapter 21

Sellers Are Liars

(Some New Rules for Advertising)

> *"... it was advertised as containing ten rooms, and he found the number eked out with the bathroom and two large closets. 'It's light enough,' said March, 'but I don't see how you make out ten rooms.' 'There's ten rooms,' said the man, deigning no proof."*
> —*William Dean Howells,* A Hazard of New Fortunes, *1890*

JUST THREE MONTHS after I got my New York license, I hit that magical point where other agents learned that I co-broke and decided to send flyers to me.

You know that old real estate adage that "buyers are liars"? I can tell you, from reading my e-mail, that sellers are liars instead. Or at least sellers' agents are. They're such liars, in fact, that I have to lay down some rules. These rules used to be practiced implicitly 15 years ago, but if they have to be delineated now, well, so it shall be:

1. Square footage is a measure of floor area. If you have a 10 foot by 20 foot room, and you put a sleeping platform in it, you have not magically created a 400-square-foot room. Really. You. Haven't.

2. Square footage is a measure of indoor floor area. A terrace, no matter how long and lovely, is not indoor space and can't be

counted as such. The big firms are especially guilty of "accidentally" sliding this number over. However, buyers want to know how much room they have for their plasma TV and their couch, not for their hostas.

3.   All of New York City, henceforth, is going to be divided into two neighborhoods: SoHo and Harlem. Because all the sellers I run into seem to think SoHo, a neighborhood of around five square blocks downtown, extends to everything below Central Park, and *Harlem* is code for "gentrifying bargain," this is gonna work out great for everybody.

4.   If I see the name of one more fake "starchitect" I'm gonna spit. Costas Kondylis, you wanna hang out with Trump, that's your business. Philippe Starck designs hotels, so people have heard of him. Everybody else, I am extremely dubious about the value their name adds to a listing. I'm going to start using the names of my old grade school teachers: "Interiors by Sally Laidlaw."

5.   In order to be a bedroom, a room has to have a window. (Also, technically, a closet, but we know that would frak up half the listings in the city, so let's just go with a window.)

6.   Because this list is probably starting to bore the people in the suburbs, let's say five bedrooms do not an "estate home" make. It doesn't have to be the Biltmore, but an estate home should have belonged to someone who rated a pretty decent obituary in a good-sized local newspaper, not just your average orthodontist in Westchester. Also, it should have some kind of sweep: outbuildings and/or a tennis court.

7.   Anything less than 20 feet square can't be a "loft." It can be *loft-like* or a *mini-loft* or *loftish*, but technically, in order to "loft" something, you first need to be able to raise your arms without hitting your bed or your sofa.

8.   A "view" indicates a line of sight. If something is in the way of the

object you would like to view, we use the words "partial view" (or we will when I run the world). Why? Because those words were invented to indicate that something (perhaps trees in the summer, or a 40-story condominium building year-round) is in front of the thing you would ideally enjoy viewing. Repeat, class: *partial view.*

9. Nothing in this world is "unheard of": not taking candy from children, not shooting the President, and certainly not closets.

10. A house or an apartment is not a "great investment"—because, as the personal finance guru Robert Kiyosaki has pointed out, a home is not an investment. An investment is something you are certain will pay off in the future, like teaching a child, putting money into an insured savings account, or sending extravagant gifts (such as wealthy referral clients) to your favorite real estate writer.

Actually, I'd say that last is a great investment. But remember, I'm a seller's agent.

Chapter 22

Homeaphobia

(Buyers' Failure to Commit)

IT'S WHAT I call "the bachelor's dilemma": Have I seen everything yet?

"Sure," the client says, "I saw some stuff that I liked. Hey, I even saw some stuff that was great! There was that one, last weekend; I fell in love with that. And could have lived with it forever, and been blissfully happy.

"But I don't want to bid on it because maybe there's something else, something better, that I haven't seen yet."

I bet clients have always been this way, but I'll venture that the reluctance is worse today than ever. And I blame the Internet; Craigslist, for one, serves up the equivalent of Internet porn, mistily lit listings that buyers salivate over and that I have to try and replicate in the cold, hard light of day.

Take this one:

Sunny Midtown Studio with terrfic city views!
Seperate Kitchen / 24 Hour Doorman / Elevator Building
Pet friendly.
Steps to Time Warner Center and Columbus Circle.
Central Park is 4 blocks away.

Spelling aside, it doesn't sound like a bad apartment. And Patty, my buyer client who was looking all over Midtown West, wanted to see it.

So I called the broker who was listed on the ad, and she said, "Hey, it's an open listing, we're not going to tell you where it is." So I asked her enough questions that I could pinpoint the building, and then strolled over to talk to the doorman.

"I'm a downtown real estate agent and I'm looking for an apartment for sale in this building," I said.

"There were two but they've been sold," he said.

"That's funny; I heard there was one available. If you hear of anything, will you call me?" I replied. This is the point where I should have handed over 50 bucks with my card, but I didn't have a fifty, and this was in Midtown, where I'm not so sure I want to kill myself to get recurring business.

So I simply jackrabbited back to my computer instead, and called the two agents who had just sold in that building. One I knew, and she told me that there was a FSBO, a listing that was for sale by owner, and also where it was. She'd seen it, and we established that it was in good condition but small (which you can kind of tell by the Craigslist photos anyway).

So I left another note the next day, this one for the seller. ("You look familiar," said the doorman.) I'm not trying to break my back for my buyer to see the place, because I think it's a little small, and the owner is asking 8 percent above the two just-sold comparables. But I feel like I have to try.

Besides, I've shown Patty nine apartments. Prewar, postwar, walkup, elevator, doorman, the list goes on. The one she should have bought was number six—she loved it and I knew she loved it. Her parents liked it. It just fit, you know what I mean? What's more, as we finished up the circuit, everybody kept circling back around to talk about it, the way you say, "Hey, remember that really great dinner we had last weekend? What a steak that was."

But Patty's not yet ready to make the jump. I'm scared that by the time she steels herself, the great apartment will be gone—not an unusual

FIVE TIPS ON BUYING IF YOU HAVE
A FEAR OF COMMITMENT

1. **Check your motivation.** Buying a home is a hassle; be sure it's something you really want to do, not just something that you feel you ought to do. As my dad used to tell me when I was a teenager: "When in doubt, don't."

2. **Up your budget.** Realize that a decent agent wants to do a deal with you and move onto the next client, so the first five properties you see should be the best ones. If you hate all of them, spend more money.

3. **Veer into left field.** If your agent is showing you what you ask for, and you're not happy, consider that you may not know what you want. So strike off in a new direction; if you love Colonials, take a look at a ranch. If you love prewars, look at a modernist glass box.

4. **Make a lowball offer.** I am generally not a big fan of these, having found from personal experience that they don't work, but if you see something you kind of like, dip your toe in the water at a low price, and see whether you get the urge to swim.

5. **Play house.** This is a concept lifted from finance guru Suze Orman (she's great, run out and buy all of her books immediately). To see what impact a purchase would have on your budget, spend a couple of months living as though you *had* made the purchase. So, for example, if your rent is $1,000 a month, and you're thinking of spending $2,500 a month to buy a place, save $1,500 a month for three months and see how this new financial structure fits your lifestyle.

fear in the market segment she's playing in, where paying $300K near Lincoln Center represents an outrageously expensive starter apartment for her, but merely a cheap *pied-à-terre* for some suburban surgeon. I'm trying to prod my buyer, but part of her reluctance to commit is the idea that number 10 is out there somewhere. The perfect 10, just out of her reach, and if she sees it that will be it, that will be everything.

Maybe I'll write the FSBO a really nice letter.

Update: While I'm in San Francisco for a real estate conference (you'll hear all about that in a few chapters), Patty finds the perfect apartment, which is actually in Chelsea near where she works. She buys direct from the owner, who is adamant that she not bring a broker in, so she doesn't—there's all of my work down the drain, though I think I left her with a reasonably positive impression, so maybe she'll refer. "They all buy eventually," says Gil when I tell him this story. With some of my clients now, I wonder what *eventually* means—is it like Keynes's "in the long run, we are all dead"?

I do take to heart, however, that she bought in the area that was her second preference, not her first. It's experiences like these that shape brokers, and are the cause of us not quite believing you, dear customer, when you say you know exactly what you want. I fully believe that if you see the right place, you'll know it, and you'll make the leap.

Chapter 23

Freaking Out

(Maybe I'm a Little Stressed)

ONCE EVERY SIX weeks or so, I have a meltdown. Why? I'm not sure. Is it biology, neuroticism, a bad behavioral pattern I learned when I was a toddler, or a character flaw of perfectionism plus stress? I don't know; I just know it has been the case since I was a little kid. As an adult, 15 years of therapy have taught me to be as self-attentive as possible: I don't let myself get too hungry or too tired. I walk away from potential fights rather than get enmeshed in them. I talk to my friends, find comfort in religion, and watch the booze.

I feel like I'm functional 98 percent of the time, so I give myself an A, but still, I can deliver a doozy of a tantrum when the mean reds strike. When I lived alone I knew it was a bad day whenever the cat would hide under the bed while I tossed shoe boxes around the room. When I had been dating Ivan for a few months, I called him on the phone at 3 A.M. and tried to break up with him, explaining that I was so angry I just couldn't let whatever-it-was sit till it was properly morning.

The thing about this kind of narcissistic rage is that it actually makes *me* feel worse than whoever else is nearby having to listen to me freak out. I feel so mad, or so guilty about being mad, that I just want to die. It's tough, in that state, to remember that the thing I really want to do is to go to yoga class.

Well, of course this kind of drama-queen behavior can't be indulged in at work. The corporate world, I learned early on, was tough because women weren't allowed to be emotional. I learned on Wall Street that you could *display* anger, sure—you got points for being able to ream someone out so effectively that they shook in their shoes—but you had to do it from a standpoint of cold calculation. If you actually *were* angry, you didn't yell at your subordinates, you went shopping. (Unless you were a guy, and filled with narcissistic rage, and then you became a managing director.)

But I digress. Every six weeks or so, I succumb to some combo of internal perfectionism and stress, and I fall through the floor. I generally do this at home, and on a good-bad day I call my friend Stephanie in San Francisco and she babies me until I feel a sunshiny kind of optimism again. On an average-bad day, I collapse on the bed, and everything just melts into the kind of tears Holly Hunter's character dissolved into in the movie *Broadcast News*. On a bad-bad day, my husband gets hit by the storm, like so:

Me: *We don't have any money. I don't have any work. I've fucked up everything. I hate myself. I've failed, and it hurts so much. I want to die.*

Him: *Don't say that, don't say that. Things will work out; didn't we find each other? C'mere, hon. And stop screaming, it scares me when you scream.*

Me (screaming): *I feel horrible. You don't understand what it's like to feel this way. I hate you.*

Him: *No you don't, and you know that.* (Lets me cry myself out, then makes a cute face, just to piss me off.)

Me: *No, but I don't want to feel this way. Also I want success and a big apartment and diamonds and a dog.*

Him: *We'll get you success and a big apartment and diamonds. It's okay, hon. Please stop stamping your foot.*

I generally do, but reluctantly. It's like I'm four, and I can't quite find the passage back to 40. At this point, all I can do is to try to paste myself back together. The trick, if I'm going to see clients, is to splash cold water on my face and eat something sugary so I don't have crying-jag hiccups.

Yet one of the miracles that I'm starting to see this year is that these episodes aren't getting more frequent—in other words, the things that used to make me batty still make me batty, but in a year of great turmoil, disappointment, and extreme financial stress, I'm not getting worse. (Though I still throw tantrums about wanting a dog.) My father, who was a psychologist, used to say that the first year was one of the hardest years of marriage, and we seem to be making it through. One trick is that hubby and I have rules for fighting, and we stick to them—for example, it's absolutely off-the-table to threaten to break up with somebody you're married to. (We codified this on our wedding program with a Jack Benny quote: "My wife Mary and I have been married for 47 years and not once have we had an argument serious enough to consider divorce—murder, yes, but divorce, never.")

Also, I try not to let my baggage spill over onto other people. So maybe I'm not making my way in the world and I want to scream, but I have tremendous reserves of patience for clients and potential clients, because, of course, it's easier to be nice to other people than it is to be nice to yourself.

It's a low standard, maybe, but I call that my equivalent of grace under pressure.

Chapter 24

FSBO Chaos

(One Apartment, Three Prices)

WHAT DOES IT mean to market a property?

I know any reader who's a real estate agent has rehearsed listing presentation answers. But stop and think about it for a minute, as though you're selling your own home—what we in the industry call a *for sale by owner* (in short, a FSBO). What would you say?

The reason this question came up is that I befriended a FSBO in my building (let's call her Daisy) and tried to help her out. I am one of those people who think that not every broker can be as great as the brokers that I love, and that if people have a poor perception of other brokers and want to sell their own apartments, well then, that's fine. I have a lawyer—okay, two lawyers—but the point is that there are professionals who charge me $350 an hour to review my contracts and draw up my partnership agreements, and yet I did my prenup over the Internet. Some things you want to do yourself to have more control, or just to save money: I get that.

So when I met this FSBO and she said she would pay 3 percent to any broker who would bring her a buyer, I threw my hat in. "Sure, pit us against each other, and see who brings you a buyer," I said. "You'll get the best service that way."

What I didn't realize is the pricing chaos that would ensue. You have, first of all, to understand two things about this FSBO: she was in a hurry, and her price was too high. These are not things that normally go together.

The initial pricing problem, one I feel like I've seen a lot from do-it-yourself owners, stemmed from too much available information. I'm all into transparency and the groovy data-filled future and all that, and I think sellers should have as much info as possible; but the fact is, whenever they see comps, sellers always pick the one with the highest price, regardless of reason. So Daisy wanted $550K for her alcove studio because the highest price anyone had gotten in her line was $550K.

There was no consideration about whether the unit that had sold for a top price had a better kitchen than her unit, or a better bath, or a better real estate agent. Or perhaps it had sold at a time in the market when it looked particularly good against its competition. No consideration of any of that. Just, "I want $550K."

"Would you take $530K?" I asked. "That's probably where you're going to end up."

"That wouldn't make me happy," she said.

The competitive market problem when she started is that there was another line of apartments in the building, with nearly identical layouts, that had a unit on the market for $535K. So right off the bat, there was a marketing problem, because the cheaper line was actually two feet narrower, but you'd have to get fidgety buyers to sit still long enough to explain what a difference two feet in the width of the living room makes, and why somebody should pay $15,000 for something that they can sense but not exactly see. But the bigger problem was that when Daisy authorized all us competing real estate agents to find buyers, she didn't declare exclusivity of channels, and she didn't control pricing.

I put her apartment on Craigslist, at the price she guided me to, $565K. Unsurprisingly, I got no takers.

When I went to check out what the other agents were doing, I found the apartment on NYTimes.com, *three separate times.*

For those of you who aren't in New York, realize we don't have one exclusive multiple listing service (MLS). There's a database called Real Plus that goes to most firms, so agents effectively share listings, but the nearest thing to an MLS that a buyer can see are *The New York Times* online classifieds. (You know that I'm an old Postie, so it truly hurts me to give props to the *Times,* but it's so.)

So how many of you see the same listing multiple times?

The first salient point is that advertising on NYTimes.com costs money. As an agent without a listing, I'll troll for buyers, but I certainly wouldn't spend good money to advertise a nonexclusive. How in the hell are you going to get paid doing that? Yet apparently at least three agents in this town are more desperate than I am.

The worst part was, the apartment was advertised *at three different prices.* If memory serves, in late May 2006 you could find the unit listed at $550K, $560K, and I think $575K (when I went to check to write a column about this, the middle agent had raised his price to $575K).

Every listing used the same photos of course, so buyers must really have been wondering what the hell was going on. I mean really! If you were a buyer, would you buy 1) the apartment described as "the perfect prewar"; 2) the unit being hawked by a "motivated seller" (the phrase I had used in my Craigslist ad, so I'm glad somebody read my copy); or 3) the apartment listed at $25,000 lower than the other two apartments?

I would go for 4) what kind of scam is the seller trying to pull?

I wrote the FSBO and pointed out the pricing chaos, saying I was going to stop Craigslisting the apartment because I thought the multiple prices would confuse buyers. She didn't respond to my e-mail.

Then I wrote about this whole situation in my column on Inman News (*www.inman.com*). My story was basically the stuff you've just read, plus "Oh, wait it gets better. I'm on NYTimes.com as I'm writing this, and those nice people at Foxtons have it listed at $549K—and they've decided it's a one-bedroom!" (To their credit, they did relist it as a studio once my column came out.)

To sum up: In June 2006, there was a free-market real estate exercise going on in Midtown. If you searched NYTimes.com for apartments in Midtown West, you'd get 85 listings priced between $500K and $600K. Four of them would have been the same damn apartment, which, like Levi's, was available in a variety of sizes and price points.

Four months later, the competition—the "narrow" listing priced at $535K—had sold at $505K. Daisy had stopped going the FSBO route and listed her apartment with one of the real estate agents competing for her business, the one who had started holding open houses for her even before signing a listing agreement. That agent ended up dropping the price of Daisy's apartment to $525K. After eight months, the transaction has still not yet closed.

Say the sale does eventually clear around $515K. If Daisy pays 3 percent commission she'll keep $500K. If, more likely, she's got a 5 percent agreement, she should net around $490K when she manages to close.

If she had initially listed with a full-service 6 percent agent (perhaps me) and priced appropriately at $539K or $535K but then dug in her heels, she would have raked in the same net return, or better. (I certainly would have taken the listing at 5 percent if she hadn't been out of her mind on asking price.) I'd argue that if she started off where a full-price real estate agent would have guided her, she would have had an easier time selling—buyers wouldn't have had their hackles raised about our building and all its weird phantom listings, and the transaction would have been closed by now.

I don't even know what moral I want to draw here: That buyers are right to complain that buying in New York is impossibly confusing? That, generally, a five foot by eight foot windowless walk-in closet isn't a bedroom? That FSBOs get the service they pay for? That I'm always right, that real estate is about intrinsic worth rather than smoke and mirrors, and that an apartment's going to clear for around what I say it's going to clear for? Maybe all of the above.

I do know that if I had been the agent trying to sell the $535K listing in this building—which as far as I know, there was only ever one of—the appearance of one competing apartment at three different prices would have caused me to go on a rampage with a gun. And I would have felt perfectly justified taking the bullets out of my marketing budget.

Chapter 25

Back to Work?

*(In Which I Am Offered What 10 Years Ago
Would Have Been My Dream Job)*

"Honey," my husband says to me softly. "I'm in trouble at work."
He starts to cry and can barely get the next words out. "I think I'm going
to lose my job later this week."

NOOO! I think. *That's not our agreement. Our agreement is I get to try this
and you provide health insurance; that's our agreement. So what if you're working
round-the-clock and I haven't made money for nine months, isn't nine months short
for an adventure?*

That's what I think. What I do is go to my computer and send out
three e-mails. Within a week I am in the offices at Bloomberg, the media
conglomerate, interviewing to lead their new team covering real estate.
It would be everything I'm good at: launching a new journalistic product
with some cool bells and whistles for an affluent, professional audience.
The people at Bloomberg are nice, and they love the company—which
they'd better, because they're there all the time. It's one of those free
snack-and-soda places, because why would they want you to venture away
from your desk just to get food?

Another of my e-mails leads me to a business publication that is dying for some editorial help. Music to my ears, they'll pay for part-time work. Maybe, I think, that'll buy me a little more time.

Our families rally around our rapidly sinking ship. My stepfather starts sending me $100 once a month; "just for little extras" he says, though I think he knows he's making debt service on the MasterCard. Ivan's sister, giver of a ridiculously generous wedding gift, offers a ridiculously generous loan. To avoid taking it, I jump through every Bloomberg hoop on the planet. I interview several times and make presentations and take editing tests to see how well I know the news of the day and do a tryout where I edit live copy. (While it turns out I don't know that Toshihiko Fukui is the governor of the Bank of Japan, I am told I have a good "news sense." I guess my experience at the #7 paper in the country counts for something.)

At the same time, I am getting ready to fly across the country to hang out at a real estate conference and moderate a half-day of panels for Brad Inman. Just as I am getting ready to exit the biz, I am prepping to spend three hours working a conference for free, because of course it's a condition of my column gig and Brad is the only guy standing between my family and the breadline. Still, it's causing a serious identity crisis: am I a Realtor or a journalist?

If there's a bright spot in any of this, it's that I have a lodestone friend in San Francisco, and I know that Stephanie will know what to do. This is the woman who got me married off, constantly cheering on the single me by saying, "There's love just around the corner; it's just that I can't tell you where the corner is." She was right once; I figure she might be right again—maybe.

Back in New York, hubby doesn't get laid off, but gets a job transfer, which is a vote of confidence from his company. The new post sounds tremendous, but how much long-term stability it promises we do not know. The nice people at Bloomberg offer me $150K, which had always been my "number" at the *Post,* but it's not enough now. My 40th birthday is coming up, and the idea of signing up for a three-year hitch at a snacks-and-soda place—it would be, in my mind, ruling out having kids. I sit stiffly in a Master-of-the-Universe glass conference room and say no. You're not supposed to talk about family issues in the workplace, but I do, using my desire to have kids as an explanation, bowing out with what I hope is a modicum of grace. *Now you've done it,* I think, *you've turned down the last real job anyone is ever going to offer you. You better get out there and make some money.*

Chapter 26

Bored of the Boards

(What the Internet Can—and Can't—Do for You)

ARE YOU MY mommy?

I just watched a spooky episode of *Dr. Who,* a science-fiction show where this odd, ghostly child keeps approaching different adults and asking them that, over and over: "Are you my mommy?"

It's creepy because the kid is creepy, it's creepy because of the insistence of the request, and it's creepy because of the repetition. Yet I feel like that's exactly what I'm doing with message boards.

Only instead of "Are you my mommy?" it's "Are you my audience?"

Having taken a listing, I now face the marketing step of trying to figure out where my customers are. And gosh, where are they?

The Internet seems like a logical place to start. We know from the National Association of Realtors that homebuyers use the Net, and we know from our own experience that it's full of information and fun. I personally have reaped the rewards of the medium's power to connect people to each other—I met my husband on a dating site.

But man, are the real estate chat boards cold.

I post on Craigslist around once a day—offering expertise for "free," as it were. I feel like I have knowledge that many posters don't have, and to me, sharing it is the equivalent of pro bono lawyering.

But that's all I can do—any attempts at conversion, or even conversation, are met with cold, cold snubs.

The guy moving to Long Beach who doesn't have a broker? He loved my tip about asking the seller to produce heating bills, but disappeared when I offered a referral to the agent who sold me my house there (I'm not even promoting myself, for Pete's sake!).

I told a Texan who asked about three- to four-bedroom rentals in New York City about price ranges, offered him a Web site where he could go directly to a luxury developer (and not pay me), and also explained to him what brokers did to justify our commission. I wasn't masquerading; I headlined my post "From an Agent."

I got this in reply, from a different poster, under the headline "Total Crap (Broker Crapola)":

{Y}ou sell the aura of "ideal and perfect". And this person wants a 3-4 bedroom in Manhattan. I don't care who they are, the 'perfect unit' for 3 bedrooms in Manhattan at minimum is going to cost $8K/Mo.

The original poster thanked this guy for warning him about my incredibly deceptive "broker BS." And the punch line is … I had given the original questioner a price range of up to $9,000 per month.

Craigslist is the worst, because readers want free information from everyone but the experts. Computer programmer's real estate advice? Obviously valuable. Real estate agent's real estate advice? Clearly crap.

So then I try other boards, and still, the vituperation I find is just incredible. For example, I currently have a couple of clients relocating to New York with their toddler. I don't know anything about toddlers, so I spent a couple of days on UrbanBaby (*www.urbanbaby.com*) to see what was what.

WHAT THE WEB CAN AND CAN'T DO FOR YOU

- *Can:* Show you pictures of the homes you're interested in.
  Can't: Convey to you how bad a kitchen or bath must be to not make it into photo rotation.
- *Can:* Allow you to pull up maps of a neighborhood.
  Can't: Let you trust a broker who asserts a certain home is in a certain neighborhood.
- *Can:* Let you pull up tax records on neighboring homes.
  Can't: Allow you to run decent comps unless you have actually been inside those neighboring houses.
- *Can:* Provide movies of new construction, complete with exciting soundtracks and breathtaking descriptions of luxury finishes.
  Can't: Let you know whether that new designer kitchen counter is going to stain or warn you whether that new designer floor is going to dent.
- *Can:* Introduce you to a community so that you can hear multiple opinions about buildings and neighborhoods.
  Can't: Make it clear to you whether that "community" is one broker with six screen names setting you up.

For those of you who don't know it, UrbanBaby is a great site for moms to get advice from other moms about schools and breast-feeding and many other mommy topics. Yet when it comes to real estate, I keep seeing one thread: "I'm a buyer and I just saw the perfect house, but I hate the agent who found it for me. Do I have to pay her?"

Wow. It would never occur to me, if I broke my wrist and the doctor was brusque, to withhold payment after he set it. Now I understand that not everybody feels this way. But there's something about an Internet post that unleashes the id: I HATE YOU HAH HAH HAH.

So why hang out on the Web at all? Well, partly to get the gossip. Because boards are so anonymous, they're valuable as a window into how people secretly see the world. It helps me to see what posters' concerns are in electronic life, so when I talk to clients in real life I have a pretty good idea what their issues are going to be. Also, I'm attempting to meet rich clients. My firm has some rentals so high-end that they will be taken only by Wall Streeters—you figure someone has to be pulling down $400K a year to throw down $10,000 a month in rent.

There are print media targeted at those people, though I remember that when I worked on Wall Street, I barely read anything. Certainly there are personal relationships that can be worked—suddenly I'm rediscovering my Harvard classmates. (In addition, my firm markets luxury properties to other brokers who are known for bringing in that kind of clientele. We don't have a storefront office down on Wall Street, but we know who does.)

But to capture rich people electronically? It's tough. I've been trading messages with Ashley, a high-end renter I met on Wired New York (*www.wirednewyork.com*) (a forum I find pretty fun, because there are a lot of architects there, and I can learn as much as I give). But it's debatable whether the gain of one client is worth my time there. In general, it's not my audience, because there are a lot of buyers who want to buy new construction condos, thinking they'd rather buy from a marketing firm (sounds classy and honest) than from a real estate agent (sounds, well, you know).

So I try not to get "eaten by the Internet," as my husband puts it. The great real estate blogs and communities here are more like water coolers than sports bars, populated by industry people instead of the millionaire consultants of my dreams. The New York media with good print demographics have electronic communities with very little traffic—or no traffic whatsoever. (Note that a few months after I originally wrote this, *The New York Times* threw in the towel on its real estate blog, The Walk-Through.)

I bet to the extent my target audience is hanging out somewhere, it's on an NFL betting site, or at a private club (maybe I should start sponsoring squash tournaments). Certainly, the publisher who creates a Web product that somehow really only lets rich people onto its message boards will make a fortune from me in advertising alone.

Unless his product is totally full of crap.

Chapter 27

The Wedding Anniversary

(Meditations on Our First Year)

AS MY FIRST wedding anniversary approached, I was inspired to reread a children's story.

When I was a kid, I loved the Little House on the Prairie books: stories the writer Laura Ingalls Wilder wrote about her hardscrabble life as a pioneer settling the West. I thought it would be kind of fun to revisit *The First Four Years,* which is the last of them; it's the story of Wilder as a young bride, and her first years of marriage to a farmer, Almanzo.

This story, which is pretty romanticized, is full of new wedding dishes and spring pony rides and the birth of their first baby. "Manly," as she calls her husband, is a dreamboat: handsome and strong and determined to succeed as a farmer, because he has an independent spirit and can't stand the work and crowdedness of town.

As the years unfold, they're a disaster. These young pioneer kids own more land than they can pay for, and servicing the mortgages is grinding. They lose one crop to heat and another to hail. Medical and child care are ruinously expensive. Manly becomes partially paralyzed by diphtheria, and their son dies when he's just a few weeks old. At the end of the book, Laura, numb with grief and exhaustion, accidentally burns their house to the ground.

So, okay, I haven't yet burned the house to the ground, but it's tough not to take the fable to heart.

The pioneer newlyweds just can't seem to understand that perhaps God did not mean for man to farm the Dakota territory; are we making the same mistake? Here we are, in one of the five most expensive cities in America, picking and scratching at what seems to be dry, dry ground.

I'm thinking this at a time when cash flow seems to have stabilized; I'm pulling in a thousand bucks a week from writing and editing gigs, which is not the fortune it sounds like but is way better than six months ago. It's enough money to keep servicing the mortgages, and I've managed to organize my life so that I'm only working on publishing half-time. A magical tenant materialized for the beach house, and his rent is helping to lighten the burden of that mortgage.

If I close a couple of transactions by the end of the year, that money will pay my taxes. And I think two in six months is doable, though I fret continually that as a half-time real estate agent I'm doing a lousy job. Paid work constantly encroaches, and the margin for error is so thin: was the buyer I called back late "the one"? What about the direct mail drop I didn't do, the Web site improvements I didn't make, the ad I didn't rewrite?

My husband keeps reminding me of the "P-word," which in our house means *patience,* the joke being that I don't know what that is. Indeed, I have only been hawking real estate in New York for three months, but the summer stretches ahead so long, and the bills are so big.

The Wilders' story turned out to have a happy ending: they moved to Missouri, where farming was better. They both took occasional work in town to help out their cash flow, but they managed to bump and scrape along till Laura's career took off—her career as a writer, that is. Their prairie daughter Rose may have been the guiding hand behind most of the manuscripts, but Laura's memoirs became children's classics and the couple lived to be 90. That's a message of hope, I think.

I'd ponder it, but I have to go show an apartment.

Chapter 28

It Starts at $10,000 a Month

(The Business of Luxury Rentals)

AT A CERTAIN price point, it doesn't matter what I say to the customer at all.

For the starter apartment I've been selling, half of my customers have come without brokers. They know very little about the home buying process, and pose all kinds of eager questions it would never occur to a seasoned pro to ask.

But for the $8,000 (yes, a month) luxury rental I've been showing, that isn't the case. For one thing, customers aren't looking hard for flaws because at this price point, there shouldn't be any; for another, at this price point, they have their own brokers to do that searching for them.

And it's those brokers I have to sell to. The other day I was showing this loft—a SoHo dream that started at $10,000 a month, and then came down to the bargain-basement $8,000, but truly has no flaws other than its mind-boggling expensiveness. I was four minutes late to the appointment.

Four by my watch, but seven by the customer's broker's, who was leaving me an irate message as I sped up to the door. From that point, I knew I was sunk.

The customer loved the place. She oohed and aahed and made notes as to where she'd place her furniture. The school district was perfect for her kid, the home-office nook perfect for her Grandma's desk.

It didn't matter—and I knew it didn't matter—because her broker was ticked off at me. I showed the wood-burning fireplace with artisanal slate hearth, the master bath spa shower you could have an orgy in, the Poggenpohl kitchen that practically still had tags on it, all with a sinking feeling. The apartment could have come with an Academy Award and I couldn't have leased it, because I knew the broker wasn't convinced.

So when the happy customer turned to me and said could she please bring her husband by that very afternoon, I smiled and said I'd do anything to accommodate her, because I knew that phone call would never come.

And it didn't.

For the next customer, of course, I barely moved. I let her agent lead the tour, and I answered his questions. If a real highlight was being skipped over, like the fireplace, I pointed it out, but I basically treated the showing like I would have a PowerPoint presentation by a corporate boss. I didn't make the apartment look good; I made the other agent look good.

At the end of the tour, he told me they were making a circuit—yes, in New York City, there's a lot on the market in this price range—and that he would put together a folder for his client.

Of course I wanted to be the top sheet of paper in that folder.

So two hours later, I sent him a follow-up e-mail, summarizing the features I thought our place had that the competition didn't. (In this niche, for example, you have to say that the kitchen has a Sub-Zero because it's a word the customer is looking for, but it's hardly a comparative advantage that your listing has a $5,000 refrigerator because every apartment the customer sees has one.)

I was especially careful, in my follow-up e-mail, to emphasize features the other agent had liked. I knew what they were because I hadn't watched the customer; I watched *him*. No one else I had shown the apartment to had seemed to care that parking was available across the street, but this agent did. He told his client that would make her feel safe if she came home late at night. To him, it was an important feature of the apartment, and he conveyed it to her in emotional terms.

Translate a detail of the product into a benefit for the customer—that's good, solid selling. All I did was remind him of it.

So what's the lesson in this for you, rich consumer? Well, the first lesson is that my phone number is 212-555-5555. Just kidding. (Though you could get me through my Web site at *www.frontporchllc.com*.) No, the lesson is that at this price point, your agent, your choice of agency, becomes even more important.

That's largely because the tradeoffs you're making are less stark: "Should I take the unit with the balcony or the fireplace?" is an easier decision than "Should I take the unit that doesn't have room for a full-sized refrigerator, or the unit that doesn't have room for a full-sized bed?"

In the luxury market, you will want for nothing, except possibly reasonable real estate fees. Everything you see is going to kick ass, often in the same exact way. Many of the units will rely on the same brand names (Look, a Miele dishwasher! Another Miele dishwasher!), selling points (a developer wants to vacation in Italy, so to write it off he hand-picks your marble), and concepts (one building features cold storage to house grocery deliveries, and then—bam!—every new building has a fridge in the lobby).

The point is, the distinctions can be exceedingly fine, and you're probably not going to sift through a mound of brochures to find them. That's your real estate person's job; you're basically hiring your agent to pre-chew your caviar for you. It's all the more important, then, that you communicate to him or her your *X* factor: The privacy? The view?

No wish should be too small. For my SoHo listing, for example, I liked that the climate control was zoned; you could have one temperature in the living room and another in the bedroom, an over-the-top bit of

PRICING THE LUXURY RENTAL

You price a regular rental by what it has: an average two-bedroom in this area costs *X*, this rental has average features plus feature *Y*, so the correct rent should be *X* plus whatever the appropriate upcharge is for feature *Y*. I think the best way to price a luxury rental is the inverse of that—by what it doesn't have: an average three-bedroom in this area has these standard features and costs *Z*, this rental doesn't have standard feature *Y*, so the correct rent should be *Z* minus the downcharge for the missing standard feature *Y*. This allows you, as a renter, to stop admiring wine refrigerators, which every luxury apartment has, and to consider how a missing dining room or a lack of parking is actually going to affect your quality of life.

cosseting that I hadn't seen in much of the competition. It sounds great on paper, and it felt great in action; but to really show it off meant having both halves of a couple present in the apartment at the same time. If you're a luxury consumer and you think, "Hey, my spouse is always cold," that's not an irrelevant or petty want. Our industry can cater to you, so, for god's sake, speak up!

Another lesson is that price is still a consideration. The SoHo loft was a condo that had been bought as an investment, and like many investors our client tried to set the rental price by first looking at his carrying costs. So it went to market at $10,000 a month, and that didn't work, and then it came down to $8,000, and bounced back up again to $8,400 when its underlying maintenance increased. I had a client offer $7,500 who was rejected; it finally cleared at $7,500, but only after it sat on the market a little while longer and the owner got beaten down.

The thing is, the kind of people who have $100,000 a year to spend on an apartment are likely to have made their cash themselves, and they are sensitive to absolute price. Aren't you, dear moneybags reader who is calling me at 212-555-5555? I knew you were. And it's okay, therefore, to negotiate a price down. The last time I went out, I saw a lot of places that started at $20,000 and had been cut to $17,000, probably on their way to settling at $15,000. You wouldn't expect, in this city, to buy a home for 75 percent of its initial list, but on a rental that might be the right place to end up. This is especially true with a condo rental, where you're paying for location and features but not necessarily the exclusivity of your neighbors. The only way you will learn what the market will bear is to ask.

After, of course, you admire the Miele dishwasher.

Chapter 29

Sneaker Technology

(My First Rental—a Celeb! It Looks Like I Might Just Make a Living at This)

THE PAST COUPLE of weeks have been so exciting, with a buyer, a seller, and a renter. It looks like I've gone from zero deals to possibly two. But let's not jinx things just yet by focusing on outcome. Let's take a look at process:

6/23, Friday. Note in Filofax: "Do everything from Thursday."

7/5, Wednesday. I head to a listing appointment where I know two competing brokers have pitched Imogen, the seller, to list at $700K. I am convinced the property should be listed at $675K, at best. This is a tough pitch to make, made worse by the fact that I can't get my laptop to work. I would safely call this my technological low point of the month.

7/9, Sunday. I run around with Patty, a buyer I had found outside my building, and her parents. We see eight apartments in four hours. I can only keep everything straight because of the detailed notes I have made in my Filofax (whoever came up with the "notes for alternating days in alternating colors" should get a Nobel Prize). It's a useful day for Patty, though not necessarily for me; one of the agents I meet indicates that he got Imogen's listing at $700K.

7/11, Tuesday. My seller in the East Village, one of my best friends, is traveling to Central Asia, and I think we're near a deal, so I hand-carry a power of attorney to her. Sneaker technology, my favorite.

Also, in a burst of fiscal responsibility, I have a long conversation with my cell phone company. Seems if I had spent $10 more a month on my plan starting in March, I would have saved around $500 in overage fees.

7/14, Friday. I run database searches for my friend Austin, who is moving to New York and wants to rent. Everything sucks. I feel so badly that I can't help my friends, but rentals are so overpriced and expensive.

Also, I run database searches for a celeb client and girlfriend who are moving to New York and need a not-ridiculously-priced rental. He, omigod, was in one of the top 20 movies of last year. She's in the industry too, though she quit acting. Let's just call them Bogie and Bacall. This lead is a gift, a HUGE gift, from Gil, because Bacall came in through a connection from her mom to one of his tenants.

I decide that I can't fawn over their fame, but that they are at least worthy of the same level of service as my relocating friend. (I later hear this codified by another broker: "Treat celebrities like regular Joes and treat regular Joes like celebrities.") It doesn't matter; everything sucks. I page through around 200 apartments and make 20 calls. I pull four showings. I fear the apartments will be small, but hopefully not charmless. E-mail to Bogie and Bacall: "See you on Sunday. Wear your track shoes. Cabs are on me but they're never there when you want them."

7/16, Sunday. Text message from seller. "I'm in Dushanbe, hoping for good news about contract." I have nothing to tell her—the buyers are still waiting for some financials I can't seem to conjure—so I counter by asking where Dushanbe is.

I meet Bogie and Bacall on the street in the West Village and we have a perfect day. Perhaps I have suitably dampened their expectations—it helps that the first rental I wanted to show them has gone between Friday afternoon when I mentioned it and Sunday morning when I went to pick up the keys. But they're nice people, they like everything, are grateful that I'm bearing homemade lemonade (temp's in the 90s) and we have reasonable luck with cabs. We see one place they particularly like; someone has shoehorned a washer/dryer and some cuteness into 500 square feet.

P.S.: Dushanbe is in Tajikistan. Near Iran somewhere.

7/17, Monday. Gil tells me the way to get the cute rental is to hand over an application check to hold our place in line. I walk it over (more sneaker technology). I spend the day working on the board package (this is just a sublease, but it is a co-op and it is New York). Bogie is difficult in that his money and records are in Los Angeles, and his normal point person—a combination business manager/CPA/protector—is in Maui. Also, I am freaked out that the board might exercise reverse snobbery against a celeb, so I go out of my way to make the financials and the character references perfect.

At the end of the day, after a great deal of faxing, e-mailing, and photocopying, I have most of an absolutely bulletproof board package. It's about two inches high, and I take a photo of it on my phone, and e-mail it to the renters. This creates a bonding moment, and frankly, the technological high point of my month.

7/18, Tuesday. We need rent and a security deposit to get this apartment. I don't understand why I ask L.A. for money at noon and still don't have it by five; don't they know how to wire stuff?

Our office fax breaks. It's hot, probably 95 degrees, and everybody's testy. The listing broker points out she has two other applicants ready to go—*where's our money?*

Finally, Bacall's mom calls. It turns out she's a broker—can she do anything? Yes, on the strength of her word alone, my sponsoring broker writes a firm check and I walk it over. Points to Gil for professional courtesy and class.

Because I'm a newbie, I'm not sure whether to write out the check to a person—the lessor who owns the apartment we're subletting—or to the listing broker's firm, so I walk it over blank, tucked inside my bra.

7/19, Wednesday. Magical, magical day. Bogie's board package is updated, his credit is good, and I think we got points for showmanship for ferrying checks around in 95 degree heat. Provisionally, we're in. All this is done via cell phone text, because of course the heat blew a router in our brokerage office and our computers and half our phones are out. The leases get Fedexed to Bogie, who is, naturally, traveling.

I feel like I'm on a roll, so I call Imogen, the woman we'd pitched the listing of, to say we're sorry we didn't get it. Still, I say, we may have buyers for her apartment; where's the listing, I ask, because I don't see it in the database? Her response is that she hasn't given the listing to anybody, that even with my inability to work my laptop we are one of two firms still in the running. She notes with fervor that the guy who claimed he had her listing is a "dirtbag." (I make a mental note to tease him when I see him at an upcoming real estate conference.)

Also, the financials on the apartment I'm selling come in. The buyer here is a lawyer, and he's picky about everything, and this will help him go forward. I send a celebratory text message to my seller.

Gil has picked up a new listing: I go over and eyeball it, even managing to upload my cell phone pictures into the New York City central listing database. This is another technology high point, balanced by the fact that I nearly break the apartment's Murphy bed when I pull it down to see if it's a full or a queen.

7/20, Thursday. Text from Bogie at 4:20: "Do I need a witness to sign lease?"

Text from Bogie at 4:23: "I had someone sign. You can white it out if need be."

E-mail from seller: "My phone has no signal; if you hear about the contract, send e-mail. xox from bishkek."

What a great couple of weeks. So where's Bishkek?

Chapter 30

The Golden Gate

(The Real Estate Conference / Vacation)

THREE WEEKS AGO, we were going broke. Now, my husband has a new job he loves, and I've rented an apartment to a movie star. So, being the crazy free-spirited kids we are, we head to San Francisco. I'm running a pre-conference series of panels at Inman Connect, a trade show that teaches real estate agents about technology. I am a total cheerleader here, because Brad Inman gave me my column about real estate and is the whole reason I have this freedom in the first place.

The conference is held at the Palace Hotel, which is the kind of grand old hotel where presidents used to hang out and now the doorknobs come off in your hands. It cheers me up just to be in the building, and in the evenings we see our friends Paul and Susan, and Gil, and Drew and Maryann, and Ian and Mary, and Greg, and Laurie, and Stephanie and Tom. Everyone feels our financial pain and takes us out, lavishly. All our West Coast friends, survivors of the dot-com crash, have BTDT (been there, done that) and are happy to try and get us through this rough patch by stuffing us with designer foodies.

Meanwhile, my hubby and I spend four days making goo-goo eyes at each other. *If this adventure doesn't work, we'll get new jobs; we can move; at least we have our health; we'll always be together.* It's pretty damn romantic, though it's a shame the bonding is accompanied by such stress headaches. Most touching of all is his faith in me, a million times greater than the faith I have in myself. Was I an idiot to have turned down the lucrative Bloomberg job? "I really, really don't want you to go back to an office job," Ivan says. "You're doing great; don't give up on this." And then he says, for the hundredth time this year, "Go, Baby, go."

The conference itself is challenging, because I have to run four panels in a row and be "on" for three hours straight. There's a lot of stuff about search engine optimization, which no one really understands except the guys who work in it, and we agents try hard to listen hard to their dire warnings that we're going to be unemployed if we don't figure it out.

What the argument basically comes down to is this: we are real estate agents because we are "high touch"—i.e., in a service business, where the mark of being good is to coddle clients—and now our customers also expect us to be "high tech"—i.e., to be able to use updated video and search to find them the newest properties. It feels like being a great French teacher who's suddenly expected to do heart surgery, but the search engine guys keep sounding the jeremiad, and we all struggle to take them seriously, or at least keep our eyelids open.

The other moral that comes through is that as freaked out as we are, customers are even more confused, because one minute a potential buyer is filling out a form on the Web, and the next he's getting unexpected calls from brokers. Sorry, customers; we're all trying to figure out this brave new world. Also, Zillow.com, the new site that estimates home values, has assumed the cultural status of a horoscope: nobody believes it's terribly accurate, but everyone secretly checks it constantly.

I get a referral from Bacall (already? I must be doing something right!) and blow off an afternoon of panels just to look for listings for her

FIVE THINGS CONSUMERS SHOULD KNOW ABOUT THEIR REAL ESTATE WEB SEARCHES

1. When you fill out a form, the data gets sold to real estate agents. That's why we call you.
2. When you look at properties on the Web, we can track your clicks. If you click on the same property multiple times, we'll probably try to show it to you.
3. When you search Google or Yahoo! or any other search engine, the keywords you use have usually been "bought" by a real estate firm. For deeper research, try to explore several of the links that come up under "search results."
4. Photos can lie, just as words can. Think about what's not in the pictures you're seeing—are you missing a close-up of the house? Apartment hunters should be tipped off by missing kitchen or bathroom shots.
5. Blogs are advertising by agents—so see what's in that advertising. First and foremost, if you're looking in a specific area, make sure the agent appears to know the neighborhood.

friend. Never try to do business at a conference: There is so much pull on the hotel's wireless networks—that's what happens when you put a thousand real estate agents in one building—that they become practically inoperative, and I spend $150 just to get dedicated computer time at a local copy store.

Then the referral slips away without quite telling me she's done. I keep waiting for her to come back, and I feel frustrated and confused: it's like the date that slips away to the powder room and sticks you with the check. I have only four days in one of the most romantic cities in the world, and I've spent the afternoon trapped in a Kinko's. This puts me in a really bad mood. *Have I made the wrong call, blowing off part of the conference for a client? Am I chasing the wrong clients?* I have a *Mommy Dearest* moment where I feel like I do everything wrong, but I've got no one to beat up but me. I later learn that by leaving New York for four days, I've lost Patty—and my chance at my first sale. *Did I make the wrong call, blowing off a client for a conference?* Frustrated, I start to gnaw on my own hands.

The conference ends and we go to stay at Stephanie and Tom's house, which is full of light and flowers and the energy of little kids. Hanging in their spare room, I feel some of the psychic protection of my parents' house. It's beautiful here, and somebody else has to worry about the boiler. When we all gather together to make dinner, I think, *I could live in this kitchen forever.*

On the weekend, Steph and Tom and their three kids—Ava, Greta, and Olivia—take us out to Fisherman's Wharf, where I have never been. I am a bit anxious the whole time, but it's fun, and we ride an old-fashioned merry-go-round. The carousel horses don't go that fast, but I still get a touch of vertigo from the unfamiliar up-and-down round-and-round. Funny, why would I find it unfamiliar, after all that has happened in the last year?

My husband holds my hand and my friends smile at me. The kids are adorable (make that capital A, Adorable). We're all healthy. Providence smiles on me, if only I could stop being self-absorbed enough to pay attention.

Chapter 31

Coffee and Condos

(Great Customer Service Can't Be Faked)

AS INFORMATION BECOMES more and more widely available, real estate becomes more and more a game of great customer service. And great customer service can be learned, but it cannot be faked.

This insight came to me this morning as I stood bedraggled in my local Starbucks—dripping with the remains of a tall coffee the counter girl had just spilled on me. It was one of those terrible accidents—she fumbled the cup with her hands, and it just went sploosh all over my laptop (possibly the most valuable thing I own) and, of course, all over me.

And, yes, I was wearing white linen shorts.

So the people at Starbucks' corporate office offered me a $30 gift card—five hours later. The people at Starbucks local? They didn't apologize for hours. At the time, they handed me dry paper towels, but not wet ones. They refused me access to a phone to call my husband. I asked for a manager, who made an incident report but wouldn't give me a copy.

Honestly, if they'd just offered to pay my dry cleaning bill and looked sympathetic, I would have been fine. But you know what? They didn't. Am

I Cruella de Ville? I tip *sometimes,* I thought. Then I thought: if I were a guy in a pinstriped suit carrying a computer, they'd decide I was a lawyer, and they'd fuss over me.

But my main point is, you can't fake sympathy. And some of great customer service is just that: having a warm reaction because it's a human reaction. If the big city has inhibited you, maybe you can learn ways to uncover it again, but you have to have the kernel of it inside you somewhere.

I just closed my first rental deal; at the first meeting, I had brought homemade lemonade. Did I do it because I was kowtowing? No, I did it because I was hot. The temperature was in the 90s, there were four apartments to see, and I wanted lemonade. The warm, human part of me thought: *everybody likes lemonade.*

I had a referral call me the other day. A renter; a thousand dollars on the hoof.

"Janet said you'd be great," he said. "Now we already have a line on a small one-bedroom in our preferred neighborhood, with outdoor space."

"I can't beat that," I told him. "Grab it."

Of course that rental didn't really exist—the ones that seem too good to be true are usually made up by real estate firms seeking to attract suckers—and now I have a new client as loyal as Lassie. I wasn't being a genius puppet master, thinking three steps ahead; all I did was think empathetically at the time: *wow, it would be cool to have outdoor space.*

The past couple of weeks I've been running around with a Canadian client. She's relocating to New York for a job, and she's in a hurry; at this point, she's ready to buy anything with a closet.

So last night we saw a condo that was okay. It was an eight on a scale of ten. It had closets, and a nice kitchen, and it was in Brooklyn, in Park Slope proper (a quiet well-located neighborhood defined by mommies), as opposed to Park Slope realtor (a dumpyish edge neighborhood defined by brokers).

But she wasn't sure about the block. I wasn't sure about the block—we were out of my home pond of Manhattan.

So I said, "Well, if you like it, you have to go back at night."

She protested. Couldn't she just buy the thing? She's in a hurry, right?

The warm, human part of me thought, no, your parents wouldn't let you buy an apartment without checking out the neighborhood thoroughly, and I can't either.

Friends of mine who live in the neighborhood have since reported the block is anchored by a little café/performance space. When I told her that, my words carried total authority—because I hadn't just made up a song-and-dance before. And all I was doing was golden-ruling it.

Don't get me wrong, I'm not a saint. There is so much that I am spectacularly bad at: my realty business is half-time, and I face mornings as though I have been beaten and drugged. Popular and lucrative new construction bores me, I get enmeshed when I wander the Internet, I don't have great organizational systems, and I am probably mean at the wrong times.

But at least I think that looking for a home is stressful, and I want only my enemies to feel stress. I am aware that people don't have to give me their money, and I am grateful when they do (or even intend to).

At one of the first office jobs I ever had—a summer internship in Boston—one of the vice presidents handed me David Ogilvy's *Confessions of an Advertising Man*. I remember very little I did that summer, but I remember reading that book. And I still remember that line: "The customer is not a moron; she is your wife."

What can I say? It was the 50s, and the world was different. Patrician, authoritarian David Ogilvy—now there's a man you wouldn't spill coffee on. Still, his words hold out hope for the small-business person: "You make the best products you can," he wrote. "And grow as fast as you deserve to."

Chapter 32

Letting Go

(The Emotional Side of Selling a Home)

ONE OF THE things that makes New York different from the rest of the country is that co-op boards, with their need to approve new tenants, slow down every transaction. For example, I listed a property in April, went to contract in July, and will be lucky to close in September.

This long cycle has a number of consequences; I think one of them is that it's tougher for a seller to detach from the property because no one is ripping off the Band-Aid.

I didn't think about this until I went to clean out P.'s property. She had moved out a year ago, and her tenant had vacated about a month ago. I had been in almost daily e-mail contact with him, trying to capture him as a client, and as a result he thought of me fondly—after he moved out, he told me he'd left a few items and told me to pick over what I wanted and ditch the rest. So I raided the fridge, took the six-pack of Stella, gave the Molson to the super, and invited the owner to either rescue or throw out the 27" TV. "I wrote your tenant after he moved out," I said. "He told me to take the TV if I wanted it, but I don't want it. I thought maybe I'd barter it for piano lessons but it turns out old TVs aren't worth anything.

FIVE TIPS TO EASE THE PAIN OF SELLING

Take a deep breath: the census tells us that 40 million Americans move every year, so you're not the only one having a hard time. Here are five things that will help.

1. Think about "oxygen for the family," a metaphor developed by Audrey McCollum, Nadia Jensen, and Stuart Copans in their phenomenal book *Smart Moves*. Compare moving to being on a plane in trouble: if you have a family, in a time of great stress your pre-eminent responsibility is to take care of yourself first, and only then will you have the emotional strength left over for your kids.

2. Try and stay connected to the old neighborhood. Think of it as a place you can still visit, not one you're banished from. Get a subscription to your old newspaper at your new place.

3. Collect a box or a basket of things from the old home that you'll want in the new: cabinet knobs, light fixtures, and so on. Remember that your buyer expects to get what they saw, so you MUST clear your take-aways with your buyer—even if you are replacing them with something that feels equivalent to you. Chandeliers, especially, can be flash points, so make sure everybody's happy and everything is spelled out in the contract.

4. Film a video of you being in the home one last time. Let every family member have a turn as "director."

5. Smells are especially important. When you move pets, give them a blanket that smells like the old place. For adults, you might want to take cuttings or seeds from the garden (again, check with the buyer, who will feel that you can't take a 20-year-old pine tree with you).

So take it if you want or leave it for your buyer. Also, your tenant left you a vacuum cleaner and some shelving."

"Great," she said. "I'll go down there with my boyfriend; we'll prob-ably take the TV."

Then I get a phone message from the apartment: "We took the TV and the vacuum cleaner. We wrapped everything up in the curtains."

I scrambled to call her back: "You can't take the curtains; window treatments are contractual."

"What do you mean?" asked P. "They're not nice curtains. Not like my nice towel bar I'm eyeing."

Oh lord, I thought. *She sounds serious.* "Why don't you just take the kitchen cabinets while you're at it?"

"Can I really?"

So then there was the discussion that the kitchen cabinets had to stay, the towel bar had to stay, and the curtains had to come back in hope-fully not-too-filthy shape. I was pretty P.O.'d because she took the vacuum cleaner—*without vacuuming.* The standard at New York walk-throughs is "broom-clean" and I knew from being in the apartment that there was *molto* dust and no broom.

"Who moves a vacuum cleaner without vacuuming?" I asked her. (Thankfully, P. is one of my oldest friends.)

"There's not much dust," she replied. "You could get it up with three or four wet paper towels."

I did, along with a dead palmetto bug the size of a half-dollar, on the trip I made to rehang the curtains. I figured it was an attachment thing, and I'm not one to criticize, as I'm the world's worst mover. Tell me to pack and I start examining every single one of my possessions, reminisc-ing over loose screws and mismatched socks before slowly dropping them in a box. But I firmly believe other people shouldn't be like this.

Besides, P. had moved out a year ago, so how could there still be an emotional attachment to the place? I decided it was time to ask one of my mentors what to do. I wrote Ardell DellaLoggia of Sound Realty in Kirkland, Washington, who is one of the great real estate brains in America and a lovely writer to boot. I asked Ardell what to do in a situation where sellers are eyeing their towel bars.

Ardell replied that that kind of behavior wasn't crazy, but merely human. "I let them take whatever and I replace it myself out of the commission," she wrote.

Oh. Good thing P. didn't have a great love of her refrigerator.

Chapter 33

Sorry I Hid Your Underwear

(When Life in the Big City Gets Mischievous)

Dear Apartment Owner:

My apologies if you couldn't find your Calvin Kleins this morning. Here's what happened:

I'm a fairly newly minted real estate agent, and to gain customers I've been showing apartments. We don't get paid for this, but we might get tipped by our boss, and we can keep any clients we pick up. So I had been showing different apartments, usually studios, and apparently I was good at it. Buyers thought I was charming, and I picked up clients and everything. So one Sunday my sponsoring broker Gil asked me to show in his building.

Now this is the building he lives in, and is, to all intents and purposes, the mayor of. He's lived there for 20 years, and probably sold just about everybody else who lives there their apartment, which isn't bad when you consider that's a few hundred apartments.

But it's also August, and he's got properties—and a tan—to tend to at the beach. He knew I needed showing time, so it works for everybody.

Except that there are four apartments for sale in this building. And it's not actually one building; it's four, set around a central courtyard. If you're not a long-time resident and the de facto mayor of the place, it's tough to remember which address goes where. I'm not a ditz, but the whole process of showing in a complex can be very complex.

Of course Gil had given me some instructions, which I only half processed. He warned me that the building the studio was in had its elevator down for repairs, and that the first floor one-bedroom might have a sleeping baby in it, and I should turn on the lights in all four apartments so the apartments didn't look too dark.

So as usual, five minutes before the open house started I got the keys from the doorman and headed up to the studio. I followed a resident in the entrance to her building, and then, woo-hoo, found that the elevator was in fact working.

That was my last pleasant surprise because the studio was a frat-house-quality mess. I opened the unlocked door and found an unmade bed. An ironing board was open in the kitchen with the ironing still on it. (I guess they don't have ironing boards in frat houses, but there were towels tossed everywhere, several people's worth.) And, the coup de gross, *a pair of recently worn tighty-whities on the coffee table.*

So of course I thought, I'm starting in three minutes. I can't show this.

Then I thought, What to do first? Make bed, pick up towels, hide half-ironed shirts? Hell, I don't even have time to clean this place up.

So I figured that hopefully most of my customers were there to see the other apartments, all one-bedrooms, and I would just make an excuse if anyone asked after the studio. I would say all the electricity was out or something.

But there's always one customer who will never believe stuff like that, and I had a horrible vision of a buyer who just had to bull their way in. I'd say, "no, no, it's messy," and they'd say, "oh I don't mind," and then their jaw would drop.

Since I wanted to guard against the worst, I quickly grabbed one of the nearby damp bath towels, and, using it as a germ shield, picked up the offending undies. I draped the towel over them and made the whole thing into a little terrycloth pile on the couch. Then I closed the door and headed downstairs to my customers.

I was right, most of them wanted to see the one-bedrooms: The one-bedroom with the sleeping baby, and the one-bedroom with the stainless-steel bathroom, and the one-bedroom on the fifth floor. There were only a couple of customers to see the studio ... in the other building.

Of course I should have known I was in the wrong building because Gil told me that the elevator shouldn't have worked—but when the door was unlocked, I thought that meant that this was the apartment I was supposed to show. Sorry I hid your underwear. I wondered later whether it was good that I'd only moved one thing, if that was more or less poltergeist-like than if I'd had the time to be a full-on cleaning tornado.

I told many of my customers this story during the two hours of the open house. After all, one needs something to say to break the rhythm of "one-bedroom, garden; one-bedroom, modern; one-bedroom, view." They thought it was funny. It made me seem kind of airhead-y (and my juggling four sets of keys and four sets of show sheets didn't help) but it did seem like an easy mistake.

So anyway, mystery slob resident, what were you thinking? This is the big, bad city ... New York Fucking City! Never leave your door unlocked. Someone might walk into your apartment and start cleaning it up.

Love,

Chapter 34

The Closing

(Wrapping Up the First Sale)

DONE!

IN OCTOBER, MY first listing (the one I took waaaay back in April) closed, and I got a check for $6,000. For the first time in a year, I am actually making more money than I am spending.

This must be the fun part.

It doesn't normally take six months to sell something in New York; in fact, we had our "meeting of the minds," the handshake agreement that the buyer and seller would do the deal, much earlier. The problem was that the intended purchaser was a grad student without terribly high assets. His mom and dad, instead of making a gift of the down payment to their academically minded son, wanted to be co-buyers. (I don't know why, because they weren't on my side of the table, but my guess is that co-buying generated a better tax scenario for them.)

So, the buyer's real estate agent needed to prepare three separate board packages. Plus, the buyers were from out of town, so they wanted to do all sorts of stuff that New Yorkers never bother to do, like read the building financials.

Just getting them those reports caused a delay of a few weeks; the buyer wanted to read the 2005 financial statements that, it being mid-year 2006, hadn't been produced yet.

Then my opposite numbers at the Corcoran Group, bless them, put together the three co-op packages. The reward of virtue? Three interviews. We had tried to explain to the board members that teleconferencing would be the way to go, but no, they wanted to meet their neighbors, so then there were schedules to juggle and plane reservations to make.

The really interesting account of all this would be from the buyers' side, as they endured nutty Manhattan, which is both disorganized (what do you mean they didn't have the 2005 financials put together by at least March 2006? said dad, the tax lawyer) and probing (yes, you do have to each submit letters of recommendation, and no, we're not going to interview you until we've read them). But it all got done, and then boom, a closing was scheduled, just in time for me to make my tax payments on the beach house.

The closing took forever. I remembered that the check part comes at the end, so I showed up late, but unfortunately, not late enough. It took the attorneys about an hour to move paper back and forth—here's the power of attorney so the son can sign for the parents, here's the stock certificate the seller can cancel so we can issue a new one (this was not real property, but a co-op), here are the taxes that New York State wants you to pay.

I had never been at a closing where I wasn't a principal, actually buying or selling something for myself, and I found even those tedious. This one was mostly watching buyer and seller sign documents, but it was fine, though boring. I chatted with my seller, I chatted with her attorney (who could be a great referrer), and I chatted with the transfer agent.

The problem was the mortgage. The seller's bank attorney showed up, and the buyer's bank attorney showed up. The buyer's bank documents? No problem. The bank had sent them the night before. But it hadn't sent the money. I guess Citibank figured holding on to it overnight meant—what, maybe another $40 in interest? (If you're a big bank and you do a lot of mortgages, it adds up.)

So we had to wait and wait for the money to come. In the meantime I learned:

- The attorney collecting the mortgage payoff had once played minor league ball, and even worked out with Ted Williams for a week;
- That it's great to be a landlord to foreign tenants, because then you can just feign language trouble whenever they tell you that something's broken;
- That people selling a million-dollar house are not above stealing maple trees; and
- When you knit and have 12 grandchildren, you'd better love making hats.

The entire thing took three hours. It was like a hostage drama; if we'd been in that room any longer, we would have become an ABC show.

Finally it all worked out, even the money. My seller P., who had brought her laptop and worked on world-changing grant proposals during the lulls, told me later that she was shocked, not just by the bank delay, but by the casual accounting of a residential closing. With half a million dollars moving around, the attorneys were adding up figures on the back of manila envelopes. "I was the only one who had a spreadsheet," she said.

An obsolete way of working, and yet good, in a sense. If everybody else had a spreadsheet, wouldn't she have been forced to sign and initial three copies of it?

Chapter 35

Out to Lunch

(Business Heats Up, at the Expense of a Friend)

THERE IS SO much work. I have two actual clients! One woman I met on some real estate Internet boards is coming to Manhattan this weekend, and I've been spending hours looking for the right high-end rental for her and her family. It's tough because I have less experience with rental units, and so I'm not confident about what they will look like, and there are a lot of "hijacked" listings, so half the time I see a posting for $17,000 I have to do a ton of detective work to find the real thing for $14,000.

Then there's the "big sale." I got a referral for a client who wants a three-bedroom downtown, which means finally I have a client rich enough to look in the actual area I want to specialize in. For Lori, I sift computer listings and make appointments; we discuss properties, we bond. She and her hubby finally end up liking the property that my sponsoring broker had suggested I show them, my two days of work being no match for his 20 years of judgment and the forward button on his e-mail.

So Lori instructs me to make an offer, and I do, going back and forth with the listing broker for a good half an hour. Me: *This is why it should be cheap.* Him: *This is why it should be expensive.*

All in all, it's a pretty good day. I am focused. I have two potential deals, nothing to distract me, I'm burning up the minutes on my work phone and I've turned my personal phone off. I am in the zone, until this pops up on my e-mail: *Are we still on for lunch today? I'm at the restaurant.*

I had achieved the state of total and complete work focus, by not checking my calendar and not making myself accessible to my friends. So I left one of my best friends stranded at a restaurant *by herself* for a lunch that was supposed to be her celebration of *my* birthday.

By the time I actually got there I was two hours late. I said a quick thanks to providence that has blessed me with friends who will wait two hours for me to get anywhere. Then, my entry line was easy: "You know what I want for my birthday? Forgiveness for being an asshole!"

We did what we always do at lunch, this friend and I: ate lightly and drank heavily, gossiping about work, friends, and news. Her boyfriend of a year may be "the one," and so there was a lot of discussion about that. It was intensely fun, not the adult cocktail party chatter I so often get at my age, but a more tightly bonded joy of sharing cake and events. Remember how close it felt to be with your best friend in high school? It was like that. Yet, a part of me kept going, *you dummy, you almost missed this.*

My hubby insists that I'll be fine with just a little more organization, that it's not an all-or-nothing "must work/must play." Still, one of the toughest things about building my own business is that I feel like when there's work, I have to devote myself to it totally, and then I feel guilty that I'm neglecting something else.

Great real estate agents, in my experience, are divas. And I picked this career partly for that reason: after years of being a corporate cog, I wanted to be a diva. When I worked for a big company, I would get depressed and schlump into my desk, and no one cared. To pull myself out of that trap, I wanted a job where wearing cute clothes and radiating energy would count for something; maybe some of that warmth would work its way back inside. Yet now, as I'm actually poised on the brink of becoming a diva, I feel … guilty.

My shrink says that my guilt stems from a fear of success. He insists that the best way to fight that tendency is to work through it, that once I conquer a few challenges I'll find that I like it, and that once I have a little success (and pocket money) I'll want more of it. Maybe he's right; maybe I'm just being nervous about having made my first seven-figure offer.

I don't expect them to accept it off the bat, though I can't wait to hear what they say. However, I will turn my other phone on while I'm waiting.

Chapter 36

The Deal That Wasn't

(Originally Titled "Jackpot!")

I STARTED WORKING as a New York City real estate agent in April. Over the summer, many things happened: I closed my first rental deal; I moderated industry panels for a few hundred people; I accepted an offer on my first sale; I turned down a $150K job in publishing; and I got the contract for this book.

That's one of the larger ironies of my life: that I stepped away from publishing only to get drawn back into it. In my twenties and thirties I was desperate to publish a book. Some of this was Harvard hubris; the people I went to college with were all writing for *The Simpsons, Friends,* and *Late Show with David Letterman,* and I wanted something to show for my career besides a handful of yellowing press clippings. I got so far as to acquire a high-powered agent (Witherspoon & Associates; you've read Kim Witherspoon's authors if you've cracked *Confessions of a Shopaholic, Divine Secrets of the Ya-Ya Sisterhood,* or *Kitchen Confidential*) and circulate three failed proposals. But after a bunch of "rave" rejections with sentences like "Alison is very funny, but..." I broke my agreement with Kim and stopped trying.

So of course when I'd chosen another career and I was out at the beach house waiting for a contractor, I got the call. The unsolicited call. The offer was roughly this: "You've been writing about your adventures in your columns, could you pull those together into a book? Oh, and because of the way our publishing schedule works, could you do it in three months?"

So I remember autumn 2006 somewhat indistinctly. (If I hadn't turned 40 and marched in the Greenwich Village Halloween parade with my friends, I don't think I'd remember it at all.) I wrote the first draft of this book in 99 days—4,000 words a week, while working half-time as a real estate agent. As much of this book turned out to be new material, I realized that 2006 had turned out to be quite a respectable publishing year. I copy-edited real estate journalism, ghost-wrote part of a New York City real estate firm's Web site, ran my Oscar jokes Web site (*www.thefelixes.com*), wrote local real estate columns for *The Blade* and *The Resident,* and got a piece in *Psychology Today*. I started Front Porch LLC (*www.frontporchllc.com*), the bunch of searchable questions and answers that supports my real estate business. The year after I quit the *Post* because I was tired, I wrote more than 100,000 words, which is the writerly equivalent of a reliever pitching 80 games.

Besides, I did four real estate deals. My business is launched, because one of my renters—Ashley, a sweetheart who is paying the stupendous market price of a three-bedroom Tribeca loft—has already referred me three times. I went over the tipping point, and it's clear that I will make it as a real estate agent. With the perfect clientele, too: the young, hipster overeducated rich. They're just like my friends, only they happen to have Hollywood money, technology money, or big business money. So far, I have drawn the sensibly down-to-earth, and I have tried hard to repay them by being sensible.

Still, the year nearly ended with a real bang. In November I got the e-mail that every broker dreams about. It ran as follows:

I got your name from someone at XXX who thinks you're the best at your job. I am looking for a condo downtown with at least 2,000 square feet with outdoor space....I am willing to go up to $4.5 M.

signed,
DREAM CLIENT

Well, that was fun! Anybody who says looking at $5 million real estate is harder than looking at $500K real estate is lying—it's easier. For one thing, the people on the other side of the deal treat you nicer. For another, it's generally prettier (though, sadly, sometimes the flaws aren't all that hard to spot). Also, my clients were willing to pay cash, which meant a fast deal without all the hassles of mortgage qualification.

We settled on a new construction Tribeca penthouse—flexible four bedrooms, double height living room, roof deck. The kitchen alone, with its Bulthaup cabinetry and pietra del Cardoso stone, was probably worth six figures; in a particularly flamboyant gesture, the developer had built in a $2,000 Miele espresso machine where you or I might have an ice maker. We were shopping in November, and planned to be in by Christmas.

We went through the negotiations—tough negotiations, because my clients knew what they were doing and had a lawyer recommended by one of Manhattan's top ten firms. A price was agreed upon and the contract drawn up and signed. I dreamed of getting out of debt and really, truly starting my business, and I wrote an ending to this book where those things happened.

And then the money never came.

Lawyers can yell at me here for oversimplifying their profession, but a contract is three things: offer, acceptance, consideration. You don't just shake hands on the terms; you have to offer something of value to seal the deal. The consideration can be symbolic—in Jewish weddings it is often a plain ring, and when my friends Stuart and Elizabeth got married, it was a pen. But it has to be there.

Yet my clients' down payment wasn't. First, it was a check to their Biglaw firm that got lost; that check was resent, by UPS, to their original lawyer. And lost. My offer to dig in the bowels of the UPS warehouse on West 43rd Street was turned down. "They can wire the money overnight, just have them do that," Gil said, cautioning me not to book that plane flight for Saint-Tropez just yet. My clients said the money was wired on a

Tuesday in December; I waited and I waited, but I haven't seen a Wednesday since. They just faded away.

I don't know what the explanation was. Because every agent in Manhattan is an agent of the seller, I specifically told my clients not to tell me. Your secrets, I told them, are not safe with me.

Of course we sat around the office making up stories. My other sponsoring broker, the ever logical Dan, argued that they needed to sell a property to raise the down payment, and the sale wasn't going through. My husband posited a husband-and-wife scenario, where one of them wanted the sale to go through and the other didn't (hmm, wonder what that says about us?). Gil and I went for more romantic and colorful narratives, with my favorite being that my clients were somehow the targets of an unjust grand jury investigation and their money was tied up in the resultant bureaucratic snarl.

It's one of those things that I bet I'll never know. Of course I leave the door open for my disappeared clients, and check it periodically, as though they were a pair of lost dogs. As time passes, though, hope fades. Damn, I was *that close*. Sure, I miss my lovely hoped-for $65,000 commission that sprouted wings. Yet the worst of it isn't even the money; it's the chance to jump to the next level without taking the stairs. I was most irritated about this when I was trying to capture a new client, a fellow Harvard alum, who was looking at two-bedroom new construction condos. "It sounds like you primarily specialize in co-ops," he said. But I do have a lot of experience with new-build condos, of course I do, I just can't prove it.

Did I mention I've had one hell of a year in publishing?

PART III

More Tips From
THE FRONT PORCH

The Four Cs of Real Estate

(Learn Your Tradeoffs So You Can Shop Wisely)

MAYBE IT'S BECAUSE I'm a newlywed, but I really admire the diamond industry. They took something that's basically an emotional purchase (*"Ooh, I like that one; it's shiny."*) and created a series of "objective" scales so the process of buying would seem more deliberative and more reasoned. To that end, I've done the same thing with real estate.

The four Cs of real estate offers a framework that allows you to step back and think about real estate tradeoffs. I developed it (and by that I mean I made it up) for a speech I gave at the first Learning Annex Real Estate Wealth Expo at the Javits Center in New York City. The response? I was mobbed. Real estate will always be an emotional buy (*"Ooh, I like that one; it reminds me of the one I grew up in."*), but using the four Cs will allow you to apply a little cold reason. What's more, while the four Cs of real estate are not intrinsic to the process, they are intuitive.

The four Cs are:

- Cost
- Capacity
- Condition
- Convenience (mostly because *Cneighborhood* didn't sound very catchy).

If *cost* is no object, bully for you; finding something the size and condition you want, in the location you want, is only a matter of time. If you are in New York and want to live in a very exclusive co-op building, it will be harder, but Steven Gaines's great book *The Sky's the Limit* shows that even those hurdles are not as high as they used to be.

What if you don't have unlimited money? How do you maximize the dollars you do have? Think about the tradeoffs you can make: you can compromise on *capacity* (and buy a smaller home than you want), *condition* (and buy a cosmetically dated property, or even a serious fixer-upper), and/or *convenience* (you live in on the edges of the neighborhood you want, or even in a different location altogether; this may involve a longer commute to work than you'd like, and possibly putting your kids in less-than-ideal schools).

Think through your house hunt this way, and it's easy to see what different decisions you can make: Mama Bear gets a small apartment in an affluent bedroom community like Bronxville, packing everything into a tiny space so Junior gets to attend great suburban schools. Young Handy Couple get out their overalls and redo their home room by room, skim-coating and ripping out cabinets so in a few years they'll achieve their dream. Pioneering Childless Gay Couple takes a chance on a marginal neighborhood (because schools aren't a risk for them), props up local businesses, and leads their friends to the new hot spot.

Of course, what each of the scales means to you depends on who you are. Families with young kids may not want to compromise on con-

CALCULATING A TYPICAL HOUSING BUDGET

Your salary = $40,000
Partner's salary = $60,000
Total gross income = $100,000

Ideal housing budget = ($100,000 × 25%) = $25,000

Housing budget = $25,000
Insurance = $1,000
Property taxes = $4,000
Maintenance = $2,000
Budget for mortgage payments = $18,000

So our sample family can spend $18,000 ÷ 12 = $1,500 a month on their mortgage. Depending on how much money they put down, what interest rates are, and what kind of loan they choose, they can service a mortgage of more than $200,000—possibly as high as $300,000.

venience, because the half-hour saved on the commute may be precious story-reading time before the darling children go to sleep. As far as condition, one man's fixer-upper is another man's nightmare—certainly plenty of New Yorkers would consider anything with three-year-old paint and a broken switchplate a "handyman special." Meanwhile, one family may feel like they're splitting the seams of an 1,800-square-foot house that another family would regard as a mansion. So the point is that there are no right and wrong choices, only choices that work for you.

That's especially true in the area of cost. Certainly, the banks will write you whopping mortgages, letting you spend 30 percent, 35 percent, even 38 percent of your gross income on your housing costs, but do you want to spend that much?

CALCULATING YOUR MORTGAGE BUDGET
IF YOU HATE MATH

Your salary = $40,000
Your partner's salary = $60,000
Your gross income = $100,000

Your ideal mortgage amount if you're rich, feel rich, or don't make housing your top spending priority is twice gross income, or 2 × $100,000 = $200,000 loan balance.

Your ideal mortgage amount if you're middle class, feel middle class, or make your home your top spending priority is three times gross income, or 3 × $100,000 = $300,000 loan balance.

I tell my clients that as a rule of thumb, they should spend 25 percent of their gross income on housing.

Generally, the 25 percent rule buys you "enough house" so you live the lifestyle that you feel fits your income, without feeling too strapped, but everybody's different. Hubby and I had housing costs that were fixed at around $5,000 a month, and there was a world of hurt when our income dropped and those costs soaked up more than 50 percent of our income. On the other hand, it was viable, for us, to pay 33 percent of our income toward housing for long stretches of time. Was that because we were particularly frugal, or childless, or a combination of the two? I don't know.

In the other direction, I am regularly on chat boards with people who make good money: $500K, $1 million, $2 million a year. I can tell you that for many of those posters, especially if they have kids, a mortgage amount of two times their gross income is just right. Rich people usually say (on the Internet, anyway) that a loan amount of three times their gross income—which comes close to my rule of using 25 percent of your income to cover your housing costs—is dizzyingly high. Maybe that's because the drive that led them to become rich in the first place led them to acquire a lot of stuff—or maybe the kids are getting ponies for Christmas.

Now that you understand your budget parameters, how do you figure capacity?

Obviously the first thought is "How many people are living in the house?" and the second is "What happens in the house?" If you work from home, you will want some place that can serve as a home office; even if you don't, in this information age you still might want a place for a desk and some files. (*The Real Deal,* a real estate-focused magazine, recently did a story mentioning that the biggest change in the design of South Florida condos—many of which are presumably vacation homes—is that developers are adding home office niches to the layouts.)

There are other questions about how you live, too: Will children of the same gender share a bedroom? Do you need a guest room, or will a pullout sofa or Murphy bed do? Can you eat in a breakfast nook in the kitchen, or do you need a formal dining room? A current layout trend is to minimize "formal" space—such as getting rid of a separate dining room—and maximizing informal family space by making a living/great room. But does that work for you?

When you're buying a place, it's also worth figuring out what capacity can be added later. Can you refinish the basement or add a porch? Bigger kitchens, more bathrooms, and better outdoor space usually add to the worth of a house. Even better specifics come from National Association of Home Builders. Paul Emrath, an economist there, found that the improvement that adds the most worth to a house is raising the number of bathrooms to match the number of bedrooms. In other words, if you have a two-bedroom, two-bath house, adding a bath or a powder room should raise the value (Emrath found by an average of 19 percent); but if you have a two-bedroom, one-bath house, adding a bath or a powder room can pop it even more.

While we're on the subject of bathrooms, think about the fixer-upper approach: to buy a house in lousy condition. As someone with a touch of experience with contractors, I'd say it's not for the faint of heart. Handymen cost money, make noise, and often demand to be let into your house when you need to be in your office at an important meeting. And then things go wrong. Before you buy a handyman special, go watch the classic movie *Mr. Blandings Buys His Dream House,* and realize that all that stuff is going to happen to you.

If you do buy a "project," I would strongly recommended Alan Heavens's book *What No One Ever Tells You About Renovating Your Home.* I had a lot of "Oh, shit, why didn't I read this before I tried to ..." moments when I read it, and I still use it as a reference. Alan points out that remodeling is never as easy as it looks on TV, where they will compress a day-long repair into four minutes, but makes you feel like you can do it.

Realize, too, that the more you personalize a house, the less it's a great investment. I have lovingly sanded and repaired my kitchen walls, and they're in better shape than when I bought them; but chances are no one is going to love the macaroni-and-cheese color Ivan and I painted it the way we do. If you are fixing-up, you must think in terms of buying a house on your budget and making it somewhere you want to live, because there's no guaranteeing other people will pay you for your choices.

Still determined? Here are three tips from Steve Berges, the author of *101 Cost-Effective Ways to Increase the Value of Your Home* and a principal at Real Estate One Symphony Homes:

1. LEARN THE COMPS. Go to open houses in the neighborhood to learn how to spiff up your house, without overimproving for the area. "Be consistent with what the market expects," Steve said when I interviewed him for my Inman column. "In less expensive houses, where there's vinyl flooring in the kitchen and bath in comparable houses, you don't want to spend the money on tile and marble. In a more expensive house, though, that's what buyers expect."

2. BRIGHT AND CHEERY. This is Steve's mantra. Take a navy-blue bedroom and paint it off-white; paint the exterior of the house; and install new lighting. "A four-bulb fixture that's a foot-and-a-half wide by four feet long is $105 at the Home Depot," said Steve, "and it floods the kitchen with light." He's talking about one of the new fluorescents, which have the advantage of being energy-efficient too. In a more up-market kitchen you might think about new incandescent or halogen task lighting.

3. THE KITCHEN IS THE HEART OF THE HOUSE. I asked Steve: "What if you have a tired house and can only fix up either the kitchen or the bath?" His response was that the family spends more time in the kitchen, so, besides lighting, it might deserve new cabinets ($1,500–$7,500) and new flooring.

While you're tinkering with your home-buying parameters, the final factor that you can adjust is convenience. What town or neighborhood are you going to live in? If you can't afford a prime neighborhood, you might look for an up-and-coming one. The quality of an area is more subjective than any other factor; you can look at police statistics and school test scores, but one person's "edgy" neighborhood might be another person's "downright dangerous." I know many New York City residents who find Tribeca dirty and desolate, despite the fact that it's currently the most expensive neighborhood in the city.

Also, there's a big danger here—you can bet wrong. If you buy a fixer-upper, you probably can restore it, and as you add a new kitchen and a gleaming coat of paint the value will probably rise. But the bet you make on an up-and-coming neighborhood might not necessarily pay off, or at least not quickly. What if that promised subway line never comes, or comes 10 years later than expected? No one has a crystal ball, especially not your real estate agent.

In general, I think the only thing you can do when picking a less convenient neighborhood is to 1) make sure you could stand the neighborhood if it never improved one jot, and 2) try to base your hunch on something. To me, the key to seeing the neighborhood "as is" is to go at different times of day: in the morning as people are going to work, in the afternoon when the kids get out of school, on Saturday night to see if there are any partiers. Michael Sumichrast and Ronald G. Shafer, in the *New Complete Book of Home Buying,* insist that you don't take anyone else's word for your commute, and that you drive to and from your potential home to your job during rush-hour traffic, which is great advice, because real estate agents live in an alternate universe where we think everything is 20 minutes from everything else.

For a pillar or post to prop up an up-and-coming area, the most tried-and-true theory is "around the corner," which indicates that housing stock on the edge of a prime neighborhood is a good candidate to get the fancy-pants treatment itself. A good Brooklyn example of this is the way Park Slope has spilled down the hill from Fifth Avenue to Fourth Avenue, as well as south over into Kensington.

Beauty, natural or otherwise, is a good selling point too: Jersey City was helped by its waterfront and Ditmas Park (and Poughkeepsie, upstate) by their supply of gorgeous old Victorian housing. How gentrified Rogers Park in Chicago is seems to be a matter of debate, but both sides concede that the neighborhood is nicer and pricier than it was and that a driving factor is its stretch of pretty lakefront.

Finally, I would use food critics as pilotfish. The presence of new bars and restaurants (especially in an urban environment) means there will be traffic, which usually brings a kind of safety, and money, which usually brings more money. Again you're guessing, because restaurants can close as well as open, but when it works, it works well. I believe the food guys found South Norwalk, Connecticut, before the real estate guys did. Plus, this research—which involves subscribing to your local city magazine or newspaper and following its dining columnist—is definitely, pound-for-pound, the most fun way to house-hunt.

How to Talk to Your Realtor

(Who Should, Preferably, Be Me)

SELLERS

AS A SELLER'S agent, my job is easy: I'm here to get you the best possible price in the fastest allowable time frame. But as Messrs. Dubner and Levitt argued in *Freakonomics,* people's definitions of the "fastest allowable time frame" may vary. So it's worth researching what the average time on market is for similar properties in your area, and thinking about how quickly you expect to sell and how quickly you absolutely *need* to sell. From there, it's a matter of negotiating the listing price.

When you're selling, it's worth adapting the old engineering maxim—"good, fast, or cheap: pick two." You can get someone to do a great job selling your house, and they can make you as much money as possible, or they can go quickly, but they can't do all three. If your price is substantially above market and you say you need to sell quickly, a good agent will turn you down. Let me say that again, for emphasis: If you need to sell quickly and your price is substantially above market, you're going to be stuck with an agent you wouldn't want to meet in a dark alley, because no one with ethics is going to encourage your delusions. No agent with any sense is going to take your business.

The other thing you'll want to do is talk to your listing agent about the strengths and weaknesses that are specific to your house. Every seller thinks the ideal buyer is a rich idiot; actually, it's a rich savant, someone who recognizes the unique strengths of your property and will pay up for them without caring about its flaws. (If you're just looking for someone to overbid on your property, you'll need two idiots, because the rah-rah buyer will have to find a rah-rah mortgage lender to support the crazy price. Unfortunately for sellers, the bank guys with the green eyeshades are not so easily fooled.)

A good agent will match your home's profile to the buyer's. A buyer who is starting a home business will see the value in a big basement space, whether or not it's finished, but a buyer who doesn't cook won't see the value in your $20,000 Wolf range.

The tough thing to realize is that the things you like about your house are not necessarily its strengths. Remember that episode of *The Apprentice* where one team combined two bedrooms to make a big, airy master? They loved the big room they had created, but to their pool of potential buyers— families with children—they had decreased the value of the house. Adults and teens love swimming pools, but 300 toddlers die in them each year, so that pool you adore is no selling point to parents with small children.

What your agent should be able to provide you here is context. What features are valued in your area? What's on the market in your price point? Sometimes the market turns all at once, and you have to make a lot of hay out of fairly slim differentials. This is not trickery; this is marketing. For example, my friend Dmitri is selling a three-bedroom house in the D.C. suburbs, and so is everybody else. It's nice that he's updated the bathrooms, but he's agreed to his agent's game plan that his slightly nicer outdoor space is going to be the selling point, and they'll start running picnic table photos front and center.

If your marketing strategy isn't working, you'll know it. If you hold three open houses and no one comes, it's either the price or the advertising or both. If you get lots of gawkers but no offers, you're pulling in the wrong people—bad ads again—or something is dumpy, and you need to look with a fresh eye to see what you can spruce up and/or stage. The easiest way to talk to your agent about these things is to set up a time frame for review *before* you get frustrated. Try an agreement like, "Let's market it at $800K in P.S. 29 for two months, and then see where we are."

Sometimes a number of buyers will be turned off by a very specific property flaw. Often, the thing to do with a flawed property is to emphasize the defect. People make fun of agents for this, advertising the "peace and quiet" that comes with living next to a cemetery, but if you went through four dozen potential buyers who were all too superstitious to bid you'd see the wisdom of it. Please, dear seller, don't take this "ugly baby" marketing too personally, because, over time, it works. I tried this on a co-op, writing a "studio with everything except a doorman" ad. I had started marketing the place as a great starter apartment, a big prewar studio with a sunny kitchen and great storage, but got sick of having my time wasted by fresh-faced female college graduates who felt like they needed a doorman for safety. When I started featuring the defect up front, it was easier to get to the eventual buyer.

Buyers (and Renters)

As a buyer's agent, my duties are different. First, a real estate agent's duties vary state-by-state, but usually we're actually agents of the seller. Even if I'm running around with you, helping you look at properties, my job is to sell (and rent) homes. But second, I'm trying to get you into the best home for you. This may or may not be the home you think you want, so a lot of communications issues come up during the search.

Sometimes everybody's on the same page. When my client Veronica wrote me an e-mail saying, "I of course have the perfect apartment on a cute street in mind!" I read it as "Greenwich Village prewar," which it turns out is also what she meant. Easy communication, happy client. At other times, there's a little translating to do: you say "parkside" and I see your German Shepherd, I hear that as "dog-friendly." Let an agent know why you're attracted to a neighborhood: Good schools? Near your parents? You like old Victorian houses with wrap-around porches? But allow your agent some flexibility too. Try to talk about how you plan to use a space rather than being too specific about the space itself. Realize that sometimes I'm just going to size you up, and decide what you think you want isn't really what you want—indulge me. Think of me as a tailor, and while I hear how you like to dress, I've seen a lot more suits than you have. It will help to remember these rules:

1. Bring in stuff you like, and talk about why you like it.
This could be listings, ads, brochures, whatever—any starting point is helpful. Ken Baris, the president of Jordan Baris, Inc., Realtors, tells me that in the days before the Internet, one of the first questions a good real estate agent asked a buyer client was, "What kind of house did you grow up in?" under the theory that if you grew up in a Colonial, they'd always feel homey to you. Now's the time to discuss lifestyle issues: Are you deathly allergic to cigarette smoke? Work late? Love quiet? Hate cats?

2. Sit down and talk about the "definitions" of a neighborhood.
First, this will help both of us read listings. When I first started working with Ann, she mentioned that she wanted to be in Park Slope or Windsor Terrace. Before our first meeting, I went through the local Craigslist listings and gave her a translation key: what showed up in the ads as *South Slope* was really Windsor Terrace, and when we saw *Windsor Terrace,* we could usually ignore those ads because they meant Gowanus.

Secondly, if you're pressed for money, a location adjustment is one of the easiest ones to make (see previous chapter). The best way for your agent to suggest a compromise you'll be happy with is to know why you like the original neighborhood in the first place. If you like the nightlife in a certain area, you might want to move only a block or two away; but if the school district you like is too expensive, an up-and-coming school in a different area altogether might be the right call.

3. Provide feedback during the process.

Tom and I had been searching for a one-bedroom condo for a while when he turned down something bright and quiet and newly renovated in a hipster neighborhood. "Great," I thought. "It's the Lower East Side; I won't show him anything else there." But I asked anyway. "It's those little protrusions on the walls," he said. Turns out that what ruled Tom's brain when he looked at an apartment was furniture placement, and supporting columns that knocked out true living room corners really bothered him. Once I knew that, I could sift through floor plans to find a protrusionless condo.

4. Walk away if you ask for something really specific and don't get it.

To follow up on my tailoring analogy, if you ask for a blue pinstripe I might show you a gray sharkskin—but I should also show you a blue pinstripe. My friend Megan, who was buying in Florida, had twin baby girls, and she told the agent that she didn't want to see any houses on a street with a double yellow line. This is fairly standard suburban argot, because streets with white lines down the middle tend to be less heavily traveled than those with double yellows. Once her agent ignored that request, Megan had the right to ditch her (explaining why, of course).

5. Tell your real estate agent who else you're listening to.

If I've told you one thing about a neighborhood, and then you ask a chat board about that neighborhood, no problem: that's just like using WebMD to reassure yourself after you've seen your doctor. But if the electronic community (or your mom, or your boss, or your uncle Al) says something that's very different from what I've said, I want to know. For one thing, I use the Internet, too, and if I see your house-hunt is taking a different turn, it will confuse me. For another, if your Web sources have information I don't (like they know where the new waste treatment plant's going to be) I want it. And if they're all in la-la-land (*San Francisco prices are heading down 30 percent per year, starting tomorrow!*), I want to be able to counter their argument.

Here's a pitfall story, from a September 5, 2006, *Seattle Times* story by Stuart Eskenazi: A Starbucks executive is moving to Seattle, and asks the people he works with for good neighborhoods. In particular, they recommend Issaquah—a 'hood that turns out to be $200K out of his price range. A quote from the rueful shopper: "I began to realize that everyone I was talking to was high up in corporate and making a lot more money than I was." Well, if his agent knew that he kept hearing about a too-expensive neighborhood, she could have taken him through it and gotten it off the table—quickly.

The most difficult sales are to multiple people: the husband likes edgy, gentrifying neighborhoods, but the wife likes gated suburbia; the student likes a young and fun building, but Mom-with-wallet likes blue-haired respectability. Still, it's usually possible to make everybody happy—but the first step is to learn what everybody wants.

6. Please try to give a reasonable approximation of your budget.
Give me a range, and I'll hit the top of it—of course you're going to like the $1 million condos better than the $800K ones, and maybe a $1.1 million unit is extra cute. Some buyers correct for this by going in a little low, offering a number that's 10 percent less than what they want to spend, so there's a little wiggle room. Fine.

But don't constantly change your price range—it tires me, and it frustrates you, and it wastes other agents' time. In an Internet world, you should already have a pretty good idea of what your money can buy. If you're a really indecisive shopper, give me your laundry list and I'll show you the listing that has it all (which will certainly cost twice as much money as you have) and then we can work our way down into your budget range. It's easier to figure out what you need to give up to make your budget than it is to creep up $25,000 at a time.

What if you're broke? That's actually okay; feel free to tell your agent. (The worst clients aren't poor people, the worst clients are lawyers.) You can have very little money, but as long as your expectations match your budget, you'll be fine.

On the other hand, if you don't want to spend 25 percent to 35 percent of your gross income on your housing costs, say so up front. Why 25 percent to 35 percent? Because it's a pretty conservative range (for more on budgets, see the previous chapter). Sure, the banks will lend you even more money than that, but 25 percent will still get you some pretty conservative co-op buildings, and 35 percent will feel like a stretch but not an impossible one. How do I know what your gross income is? Your job title, your car, your clothes, your watch, your girlfriend, your expressions, your dog, where you live now—and that's before you hand me your Social Security number so I can run your credit, or talk to one of the mortgage lenders I just happen to know. If you have money, your agent will find it, so if you don't want to spend it, tell him or her.

7. Come up with an idea of what you're going to see, and over what time frame.
Remember: *Agents will try very hard to show you the best stuff first.* Gil sold me my first apartment in two and my second in four. To buy a suburban house, where I was outside his magic sphere, I had to look at eight listings. Eight! The thought still tires me. If you see more than 10 homes, either 1) you have a truly lousy real estate agent, or 2) you're jacking around. The only people who should have to look at dozens of homes are buyers with kids who feel torn between different school districts or relocators who feel shocked by the impact of the transplant. If you expect to see 30 listings as part of the process, warn your agent so she can pace herself.

8. Realize that I can't talk about certain issues of race and ethnicity.
They probably call it Chinatown because Chinese people live there, but I can't send you to a "Chinese neighborhood" or a "neighborhood with fewer white

---

FIVE QUESTIONS TO ASK YOUR AGENT

1. What would you do if you were in my shoes?
2. What's the worst mistake you think I could make? (If the answer is "not buying immediately"—run!)
3. Can I talk to one of your previous clients?
4. How many clients are you working with now, and what are you doing for them?
5. If I don't work with you, which of your competitors would you recommend and why?

---

people"—that's called *steering,* and it's illegal. What I can do is show you properties in different neighborhoods and let you pick what works for you.

What's sad is that despite the laws on the books, discrimination continues apace. A recent study by the National Fair Housing Alliance found that on average, black testers were shown fewer properties than similarly financially qualified white testers. (The study included Atlanta, Chicago, Detroit, San Antonio, and the New York suburbs.) If you're a minority, realize that's how you're being shafted: in what you don't see. If you're interested in a specific neighborhood, make a point of telling your agent that. If that agent doesn't want to show it to you, get a new agent.

LEARN HOW TO BREAK UP

When I first started trolling for clients, I went to the chat boards at *www.urbanbaby.com.* I figured that, because new moms need more space, that must be a good place to get business, right?

FIVE QUESTIONS YOUR AGENT IS NOT GOING TO HAVE AN HONEST ANSWER TO

1. **What do you think is going to happen to the market in the next six months?** If the Federal Reserve doesn't know, why would a broker?

2. **What do you specialize in?** Somehow, even an uptown agent will invent a connection to the downtown neighborhood you're looking for.

3. **Which place would you buy?** If you, dear buyer, have seen only a couple of things, I am showing you my best, and I think you could buy either of them; if you've seen a lot of things, I think you are crazy, because I think you should buy something you passed up five showings ago.

4. **How long does it take to buy a home?** I can find you a home in a day—but lenders, inspectors, and sometimes co-op boards are also involved. Most importantly, how much of a pain in the tail are you?

5. **Is this home a good investment?** Another I-don't-trust-you-but-hey-predict-the-future question. If a stockbroker can't honestly tell you that about a stock, how can I tell you that about a loft? I can make an educated guess, but that's it. All I know for certain about a property is whether you can fit a sofa into it.

Then I found that approximately every other real estate question was, "I hate my broker; do I have to pay her?"

Why this board in particular attracts this question I'm not sure, but because lots of moms ask it, I feel you should be prepared to ask it too.

If you're a seller, when you list your home, make sure you understand the time limit of your agreement, and whether there's a slope period after the agreement expires when you might still owe your agent a commission. Very importantly, clarify what happens if you bring in the buyer—whether you pay commission in that scenario is a point that you can, and should, negotiate.

Next, clarify what you expect your agent to do: Buy newspaper advertising? Troll on chat boards? Put up yard signs? Hold open houses? Throw cocktail parties? Skywrite? Anything is possible, so go over a game plan of what results you expect and how you expect to get there. (See the section for sellers, above.) Then, outline a way out if the game plan is not being followed.

If you're a buyer, you can put in an offer on the place you like using any broker. It's expected that if a broker finds a home for you, you will use him or her to put in the offer. It is also expected that if a broker schleps you around for weeks, educating you about the market and providing access to properties, that broker has provided a service to you, and that you should use him or her to put in an offer, even on a place that he or she did not directly hook you up with.

Of course you don't *have* to, and enough people don't that I think in 10 years we'll see hourly pricing for buyer's reps, so that you could pay me $500 and pick my brain about the market and then go your merry way and we'd both be happy.

But in current market conditions it's highly unlikely that the seller is going to suddenly say, "Hey, you're not using a broker, so I can cut the price by 2 percent and pass the savings on to you!" It's more likely that you are depriving yourself of your broker's services during contract negotiation and closing. Moreover, you will generate bad shopping karma, and for the next five years you won't be able to find a pair of decent-fitting shoes. I swear this is so. A long-established neighborhood broker will never forget that you screwed her out of $10,000, and she'll make sure that rebounds on you by pointing out every single tiny flaw of your home to her clients when you decide to sell.

Now This Is Living

(A Meditation on the $10 Million Home)

I REMEMBER MORE than a decade ago, when real estate cost less by a factor of 10 than it does now, hearing Gil say, "There's nothing wrong with a $2 million apartment; it's perfect!"

No one would say that about a $2 million apartment any more, no matter how much some of us might want one. In fact, it's been three years since Nadine Brozan of *The New York Times* wrote a disquisition that no one would say that about a $10 million apartment any more.

Which is too bad, because nearly 200 of them are on the New York market. About a third of those are townhouses, but nearly two-thirds aren't; there are more than 100 ways to spend $10 million on a home and still have to share walls with your neighbors. (I guess when they start to eavesdrop on you, you'll know that the glass pressed against the wall is Baccarat.)

Does that mean there are no more cool properties? Absolutely not. There is a point—a nearly unimaginably expensive point but a point nonetheless—where a home starts to have everything a non–movie star would want in terms of bedrooms and bathrooms, outdoor space, closets, moldings, and location, where one could make it bigger and possibly more like Versailles but not really any better.

Yet the most kick-ass properties I've seen aren't like that, either. Partly because at that level of extravagance, decoration is at least as prominent as architecture. Magazine magnate William Reilly has a gorgeous oversized townhouse on Gracie Square, an 8,779-square-foot place with 65-foot frontage that he affectionately refers to as a "New York City double-wide." I remember that the house was fabulous, but it was still overshadowed by his art collection; it was like the Met with closets. The Getty pad in the Pierre? I don't remember the moldings, I remember the Basquiat. The home-cum-gallery thing is so expected at the upper price points that brokers simply rent art. I remember that at an opening party at 165 Charles, a recent Richard Meier building, we were handed a little flyer that served as a museum catalog—those abstracts are by Shirazeh Houshiary, and the Ross Bleckner's in the hallway.

So in these go-go times, what makes a trophy a trophy? I propose a list:

1. *Multiple gatekeepers.* Anyone can have just one doorman. The guy-handing-you-off-to-another guy (big in the swanky parts of the Upper East Side, and in the Dakota) raises the game to a whole 'nother level. Whenever I'm a guest in these buildings, I get nervous just trying to figure out how many people I have to tip for getting me a cab.

2. *Multiple buildings.* Manhattan's all very well and good, but a good old-fashioned Fairfield County cluster of outbuildings may even be snootier. Extra points for Greek Revival so thorough that you might confuse the pool house for a private bank and trust.

3. *Views without impingement.* John D. Rockefeller's stroke of genius as a patron of The Cloisters? Buying the Palisades so that the views across the river would never be spoiled. I know The

Cloisters isn't technically a private residence, but let's admire the style. It takes money and vision to buy an adjoining lot, and it takes exceptional money and vision to buy an adjoining lot in another state.

4. *Top location.* By that I mean, literally top. The Chelsea Mercantile is a condo formed from a collection of prewar buildings that new floors were plopped on top of, with the result that some penthouses are higher than others. I went with clients to look at an expensive one, and told the broker we were also interested in a cheaper one. All he had to do in reply was point down at it. The house on the hill always wins.

5. *The latest gadget(s).* This requires a lot of homework on the part of developers, who might spend tens of thousands of bucks adding rain showers and light-show tubs only to find out that those are so last year. The current fashion in Manhattan condos is sybaritic bathrooms with tubs and showers big enough for three people to have sex in, and I'm sure in five years we'll look back at that as a lapse in taste worthy of the '80s. (*Damn all that meth, what were we thinking?*) Currently, I'm blown away by in-floor HVAC, Crestron touch-pad control systems and anyone who builds a $2,000 Miele espresso machine into the kitchen, but I'm sure that stuff will all seem cheap and hooker-y by the time this book comes out.

6. *Naming.* I can't beat the humorist Henry Alford, who decided that apartment buildings with names were more impressive and so began a campaign to name his building the Henry Alford. But, dammit, buildings with names *are* more impressive. I'm sure the Manhattan townhouse that financier Chris Flowers just paid $53 million for would have gone for only $52 million if it hadn't been called Harkness House. That just sounds rich.

7. *Weird and/or scarce materials.* At one luxury conference I went to, panelists were talking about "fir floors." I went back to my office

and Googled "fur floors"—in a world where leather tiling (which is a bitch when it gets wet, as floors are known to do) is making a comeback, fur didn't seem inconceivable. We're seeing a trend now in haute white plastic, for those of you who want your bathrooms to match your iPod. Knowing what we know about the disappearing rain forest, it would be way too Great White Hunter to buy mahogany molding for your house now, but if you bought a 1920s-era Rosario Candela apartment that had it already, well, how cool would that be?

8. *Exclusivity.* The *New York Post* called Fisher Island, Florida, America's "richest town"—the kind of private community where you can buy a private villa and then spend six figures joining the private club so you can meet your neighbors. The residences aren't actually that over-the-top—the idea of a 710-square-foot $1.4 million one-bedroom doesn't particularly strike fear into the heart of a New Yorker—but who cares when there's a private airstrip?

9. *Relentless theming.* Larry Ellison's $25 million tea house? Only seven bedrooms, but dammit, on message: shoji screens, tatami rooms, and a koi pond. Money.com's display headline was "Samurai Sold Separately." Speaking of outbuildings, the bath house was designed by a Zen monk. Makes you feel your kitchen contractors are a little inadequate, now doesn't it?

10. *Sheer effing bigness.* I give my husband Ivan full credit for coming up with the word *bignormous* here. Hearst Castle has 56 bedrooms and 61 bathrooms. The wrought iron doors in the entrance foyer of The Breakers, the Vanderbilts' summer home in Rhode Island, weigh two tons. The Biltmore estate, built in North Carolina for one of the Vanderbilt sons, has four acres of floor space. I figure I live in one-third of 1 percent of that—but think how much easier that makes the relentless theming.

Constant Renovations

(A House Is a Series of Leaks Held Together by Gutters)

I HAD HEARD for years that owning a house was scary, but I had renovated a bathroom in an apartment, which perhaps made me overconfident, so I bought a house. Finally I've learned, after five years of living in a house, that it's not that houses are scary; houses are impossible.

Houses stand outside, all day long, in water and wind, which are tireless enemies. Older houses were built by craftsmen who spent years mastering their trades in order to send their kids to medical school; finding someone to replicate that quality of work now is both frustrating and expensive. And new houses? Well, they don't build them like they used to.

Buy a cell phone, a TV, a car, and your purchase comes with an owner's manual—a description of parts, an explanation of basic systems, and a warning to stop you from doing the two or three things that will break your new plaything. A house comes with none of those things. My home inspector tried to help, letting me follow him around and pointing out various valves, but it's sort of like looking at a city from an airplane: when you're on the ground, you may remember that view, but it doesn't really help you find City Hall. What's more, inspectors are supposed to be objective, which means they can't be (or even recommend) contractors. Imagine going to a doctor for a physical, and being told you had high blood pressure, coronary artery disease, and a kidney problem that you really should get taken of immediately, but then being told that he can't possibly refer you to a specialist. It's daunting.

I tried, like every good homeowner, to take care of things a little at a time, but inexperience means it's hard to know what to let slide. The guys who did a great job cleaning my fireplace did a horrible job repointing my masonry. There's cement oozed up between the bricks, it looks horrible, and will clearly have to be redone—but by whom? Do I test out contractors by seeing who does a lousy job cleaning my fireplace? When I bought the house, I was told that my roof was fine; no worries. Once I owned the house, one gutter guy told me that my roof was fine, another that my roof was in bad shape—who to believe? I wasn't going to go up there. I learned who was right (and finally replaced the roof) when it started raining inside my house. I called three roofers, got estimates, and used the one recommended by Gil's mom, an area broker. The roofer I used did a great job; he was fast, efficient, and the leaks stopped. I was thrilled until another contractor pointed out a bit of the job that the roofer had simply left undone, slipshod. So now I use one specialist to point out the previous one's mistakes, but they all disagree: three heating specialists, three different answers.

I do know that when I bought the house there was a little bit of mold in the basement, and now there isn't—$20,000 later. The finished interior of the basement—walls, kitchen, bathroom, and closets—was entirely ripped out, which I figure also stripped the house of $50,000 worth of value. On the other hand, it's now easier to see what foundation work I need, and I bet I have one of the few houses on Long Island that has its "mold papers." Of course there's an occasional spot of mildew in the bathroom—I have three male tenants, so the standard of cleaning isn't terribly high—but it causes me to shake and cry and go to war with the

Clorox bleach pen in a way I never did before. If only, I think, I had had a manual.

So my first piece of advice is this:

#1: Marry a plumber.

#2: You will never understand your house, but you do have to attempt to care for it anyway. Think of it like trying to tame a wild animal: you'll try some things, everything will seem to be going okay, then it will throw some sort of raging, eye-rolling, claw-baring fit and you'll have to start again.

#3: Water is your enemy. Make sure water does not get from the outside to the inside of your house, even if it means you have to waterproof your stucco, even if it means you have to redo the landscaping around your foundation, even if it means you have to learn what a soffit is. Hire someone to clean your gutters spring and fall, because if they get blocked up that water lands on your roof and finds a way through to plink on your little head.

#4: Fires and explosions, when not in a Tom Cruise movie, are bad. Drain your boiler or your house will blow up (as I type this, I'm getting nervous that I haven't done this recently). Clean and cap your chimneys. Make sure the pilots on your stove are lit.

#5: Tilty things aren't good. Do not buy a house with sagging stairs, because they're often a sign of worse foundation problems underneath. Just gotta have that precious old Victorian? Okay, but first imagine serving tea and cookies to the crew that's using hydraulic jacks to prop up your porch. Buy the place only if you can embrace—and afford—that vision.

#6: Just because quality old materials are tough to replace is no reason to go for newer materials, which have their own drawbacks. For example, I like old-fashioned wood floors. I can feel the weight of the entire flooring industry coming down on me here, but I've heard too many complaints that bamboo floors dent and engineered floors scratch. In my mind, they're floors, and they're supposed to take a pounding, literally—

who wants them to be delicate? Similarly, just because it's tough to get a good plasterer is no reason to install a dropped ceiling. Just make good old-school materials part of your housing budget.

#7: Designers and architects are worth it. Even with wine coolers and warming ovens, there are only so many configurations of kitchen appliances, and other people have road-tested them already. Go ahead and hire a pro, who will help you skip ahead from your imaginings straight to what they know works. P.S.: union labor is worth it too.

#8: Always wear a better mask than you think you need. If you think you don't need anything, wear a dust mask; if you think you need a dust mask, wear a chemical respirator; if you think you need a chemical respirator, hire out the job. Today I forgot to wear a mask while using Lime Out on the bathtub, and now my fingers are so heavy I can barely type. Your home is not worth losing your lungs over.

#9: It never ends. First, renovations really do always take longer than you think they will, especially if they involve you not having access to your own refrigerator, bed, or toilet. Secondly, owning a home is like painting a bridge—you start at one end, work your way all the way through to the other, and boom, you have to start over again. Just shrug your shoulders and accept that the alternative—living in a home with outdated, possibly nonworking appliances—is worse.

#10: Prepare to clean up, because no one else will. The day after I installed a new door, the floor guy got sealant on it. I should have put protective tape on it, but duh, I assumed he would. So arm yourself for any renovation with a truckload of tarps and a Dyson, and expect that you'll be the one using them. Even if your crafstmen could recreate the Sistine Chapel, you'll find they can't work a broom.

But then, maybe Michelangelo couldn't either, or maybe he was just too busy enjoying his new kitchen.

Credit Score Myths and Facts

(Surviving a Three-Year Fight with Citibank)

ONE DAY THREE years ago, when I was still a real, solid corporate citizen, I paid my mortgage. I wrote a check from my checking account (Citibank, part of Citigroup, one of the top five banks in the United States) to my mortgage servicer (Citimortgage, part of Citigroup, yadda yadda yadda). And the left hand didn't know what the right hand was doing: the mortgage servicer took the money and put it in the wrong place. So my checking account was down $1,600, and my mortgage company was convinced I owed them $1,600.

This is the kind of little slip that takes three years to correct. (If I was one of those women who always has two clean matching socks, I probably could have done it in one, but I am the kind of woman who has one clean sock and goes searching in the laundry basket for its mate like a dog digging for a bone.) I called Citibank and I wrote them letters, and I pulled documents and I wrote them more letters. I finally got a piece of paper, which ranks in value near my passport and my marriage license, saying that it was all their fault and I was allowed to tell the credit reporting companies so.

I knew this escapade (and my year's adventure of having $10,000 sitting on my credit card as permadebt) had hurt my credit score, so I was determined to fix it. In the process of trying to rebuild that, I learned that just about everything I thought I knew about credit reporting was wrong.

Sure, the #1 tip is "pay off debt, pay off debt," but below is some other stuff you may not know about credit reporting. Your reward for sifting through the detail (provided by the wonderful Craig Watts of Fair, Isaac and Co., the people who generate your FICO credit score, and Norm Magnuson of the Consumer Data Industry Association, or CDIA, the trade association for the credit and consumer reporting bureaus) is that it just might save you some money.

Myth: You are the captain of your own credit.
Fact: There's no distinction between the person who applies for the card and any other person who can use it. If someone else sticks you as an authorized user on their credit cards, their credit history begins to affect yours whether or not you even know you're on those cards. The good news, parents, is that you can start a 16-year-old kid as an authorized user on your cards, and begin to establish a credit history for that teenager; the bad news, kids, is that if your parents have a poor credit score, it will start to taint your spanking-new credit record.

Myth: You can get credit in just about any name, so it doesn't matter what name you use on your application.
Fact: It's important to be consistent in your application so you don't create a "splintered" file. "When you tweak your personally identifying info, it's hard to track down in that base of 210 million people," says Magnuson. If your name is Robert but you go by Bob, pick only one designation as the name you carry your credit in. Don't drop generational signs, such as "Jr.," and don't guess at your Social Security number if you can't remember it.

Women who marry or divorce should tell their lenders, and the credit reporting companies, about any name changes.

Myth: How long you've been in your current job matters.
Fact: "Not a bit," says FICO's Watts. They use a score based on your credit patterns to predict what you'll do in the future, and how long you've been employed isn't sufficiently predictive of anything.

Myth: You can't change your mortgage rates.
Fact: You should look at your credit report two months before you apply for a mortgage, says CDIA's Magnuson. If your score is being dragged down by inaccurate information, that will give you time to correct it.
In the other direction, your mortgage lender will check your credit score more than once during the loan process. So once you've applied for a loan, don't do something that will cause a stream of new credit inquires—in other words, if you've got an outstanding mortgage application, don't buy a new car. It will hurt your credit score, and possibly raise your mortgage rates.

Myth: You can't fix your credit.
Fact: You can, indeed, reason with a credit bureau, though you'll have to keep your correspondence plain and to the point, and keep great records of your communications. "Simple and documented," says Watts, is the way to go.

Myth: Getting a new credit card always hurts your score.
Fact: The FICO score gives weight to your having a mix of different kinds of credit. If you have installment debt (e.g., a student loan) and no revolving debt (e.g., credit cards), adding a credit card may well help your score rather than hurt it, says FICO's Watts.

Myth: To improve your FICO score, close some credit cards.

Fact: The credit score model checks what percentage of your capacity you're using—both overall and on each individual card. If you have one maxed-out card, that hurts your score, but closing an empty card won't help you. The trick is to get your debt use below a certain percentage of the capacity *on each card*. CDIA's Magnuson suggested one-third as a rule of thumb.

Myth: Once you've declared bankruptcy, you're screwed.

Fact: Bankruptcies do stay on your report for a long time, up to 10 years in the case of Chapter 7, 11, or 12, according to the Web site of credit report agency Experian. But you can re-establish good credit faster than that; "in three or four years," says Watts. The important thing to remember with your new accounts is to pay on time, always. Time will heal even self-inflicted wounds; the past two years of your payment history are always the most important.

Myth: If you shop around for a mortgage rate, that hurts your credit score.

Fact: Perhaps in the past, but not any more. As long as you make all your inquiries within a month, it's not going to hurt you to shop around, says Watts. You want to get the best loan rate? Go ahead and call all the lenders you want.

Home Comforts

(Secrets to Coziness That Should Be Revived)

MAKING A HOME warm, gracious, and comfortable is not an easy thing—but it's not that difficult, either. The main thing it takes is effort on both an emotional and physical level; you have to dream what you want your house to be, which can be scary, and then you have to get it there, which takes work. Still, the work doesn't have to be painstaking—if you want to be a Martha with a garden calendar and iced cookies for all seasons, go for it, but busy doctors should find something useful in the list below too.

Here's the secret: a gracious home is not an all-or-nothing proposition. You can create a lovely reading nook in the midst of clutter, or whomp up a focal point even if you can't manage to do the dishes every day.

The argument that tending to your home, even a little, can have a gigantic payoff isn't one I was raised with. I was the latchkey child of two working parents; my nanny, Dorothy, taught me how to be a good person, but I didn't pay that much attention about how to dust. Even in my mid-twenties I used the floor as a filing system, until I read Cheryl Mendelson's *Home Comforts,* the book that lends this chapter its title.

Mendelson argues that the decision to commit to your home, the decision to really live in it, can have incredible rewards. Imagine wanting to come home, wanting to turn the key and enter your own little groovy place. So that's the philosophy. Because I'm lazy, I've adapted it. Here are 10 little nuggets to try:

1. Make a beverage habit into a ritual.
Chances are you drink something: coffee in the morning, tea in the afternoon, wine at night. If this is a daily or even a weekly habit, why not get pretty accoutrements? And shouldn't the supplies have their own shelf? In my first New York studio (12 feet by 20 feet, with a 5-foot by 5-foot kitchen) I hung a little ledge for the coffee grinder, the Melitta cone, the box of filters, the scoop, and a couple of mugs. It gave me a little point of order to the kitchen. You can add rituals of time, too (on birthdays, drink champagne out of Grandma's glasses) or for relationships (when Stephanie and Tom come over, pull out the good Scotch).

2. Acknowledge the seasons.
You don't have to go crazy and hang red-white-and-blue crepe paper for Washington's birthday, but it's immensely satisfying to have a pumpkin in the house in the fall and a vase of lilacs in the spring. To make this most effective, don't overshoot: If you go to the beach in the summer, you can bring shells home as souvenirs, display them for the season, and then (I know this is radical) throw them out. The point is not to kitsch up your place—don't fall into the who-has-the-most-Christmas-lights competition mode—but just to bring small touches of the current outdoor environment in. If you're religious, responding to the calendar will tie your home and spiritual life together, but even if you're not, a dash of seasonal decorating can be quite calming. You may think, "I'm too busy to do that," but embracing time can make it seem to slow down as well.

3. Follow the sun.

It can be tough to yank the curtains open in the morning—but getting that eyeful of sunlight helps "set the clock"—it regulates your circadian rhythms, and it translates to better sleep. You should dim the lights about an hour before bedtime too. If you're feeling handy, installing a dimmer switch requires only one bit of specialized knowledge (the ability to find your circuit breaker to temporarily shut off your electricity), and should take you 15 minutes, tops.

4. Create a reading nook.

A reading nook is really just a space with three elements: a comfy chair, a task light, and a side table (which can hold your cup of tea). The table, and especially the chair, are up to you: beanbags are popular for kids, rattan for recent grads, and rolled arms or wings tend to grace chairs for grown-up people.

There is, however, a math for the reading light, courtesy of E. W. Commery and C. Eugene Stephenson's *How to Decorate and Light Your Home,* a 1955 publication with General Electric ties that tells readers how to "live better electrically." To place a floor lamp, sit in your chair, open your book, measure 15 inches to one side from the center of your book, and measure at a right angle 26 inches back. That's where the center of your lamp should go; the height should be around four feet from the floor to the lower half of the shade. Try this, it really makes a difference. To place a table lamp, take the center of your book, measure 20 inches to the side, and make a right angle 16 inches back; that's the center of your light. The lower edge of the shade should be from 39 to 42 inches from the floor, depending on your height. Three-way bulbs, I find, are best.

5. Form a gathering place.

The notion of where the communal space in a house is changes over time; that's why today, a 1970s house with a wet bar seems dated. The important thing is to find a gathering place that works in your particular home, a place where kids and company alike feel welcome, and then play that up.

In our beach house, we put a wooden garden bench ($90) and two Ikea pillows ($10 each) in the kitchen, so guests can chat with us while we cook. Other possibilities include throwing a futon couch in a semifinished basement; putting pillows on the rug in a dorm room; or adding a chair a year to your dining room set until nobody is sitting on folding chairs for Thanksgiving.

6. *Heat-treat your sheets.*

I owe this one to Carol Mendelson, the idea that pillows are full of dust mites and that the best way to kill them is to launder your sheets, pillowcases, and mattress pad in hot water. Relief is instant; try it once and you'll wonder why you put up with having the sniffles all those years. To be effective, you have to use hot, not warm, water, so make sure your sheets can stand up to the pounding. If not, buy cheaper cotton sheets and wash the bejesus out of them.

Oh, and while we're on the bed: your duvet cover should be one size smaller than the duvet.

7. *Frame something.*

One thing we've learned from the staging mavens is that every room should have a focal point, something that draws your eye, hopefully set up to capture your attention as you enter through the doorway.

While that can be many things—furniture, an architectural detail, a decorative vase—one of the easiest is wall art. Pick something that's important to you and that you want to see over and over again. Photos are always a good go-to; my friend Peggy Lou just had her first kid, and a two-foot by two-foot blow-up of the baby is propped above a bookcase in the entrance hall. I also remember the lovely feeling of a friend's parents' rec room filled with 5×8 vacation snapshots, with the destination and year written on each photo in silver marker. The journey from "Bahamas, 1958" to "Paris, 2006" told the story of a marriage.

8. Polish something.

A woman named Marla Cilley, who calls herself the Fly Lady (*www.flylady. net*), has practically started a new housekeeping wave. The first step in Cilley's method is to "polish your sink"—her book is called *Sink Reflections*—and the point is not that cleaning your sink is the most important housekeeping task but that it's rewarding to be able to smile at yourself. (Are you feeling the "because you're worth it" vibe yet?) I would argue that you can get the same kind of high off of Windex and your bathroom mirror, or a polish cloth and silver vase. I get happy every time I tackle the chandelier. So go clean something shiny (for heaven's sake, not the dishes).

9. Create a staging area.

I recently saw a $2.7 million penthouse: a classic prewar building with great views of Greenwich Village, but the thing that impressed me most was the original key shelf built into the coat closet. Now that's thinking. Imagine how happy you would be if there were a place, preferably near your front door, where you always put your keys and wallet and cell phones. Think what a great emergency resource it would be if there were a fire and you had to find those things in the dark. Now get a hammer and hang one of those little valet things on the wall. For those who are intimidated by even that: knock on the wall and you'll hear sounds that are "more hollow" and "less hollow." You'll want to put the nails into the wall at the less hollow sounding places, which are the wooden studs behind the wall, 16 inches apart. If you have plaster walls, clear off a table and put a tray down.

10. Care for something that has different life-rhythms than you do.

I look forward to getting old and being one of those crazy animal lovers that has dog biscuits falling out of the pockets of her housecoat. But I think even if you're not a crazy dog-lady (or cat-lady) in the making, there's value, to you, in caring for anything that has life-rhythms different than your own. For one thing, it makes you the master and caretaker in your own home, which is a great counterweight to an out-of-control closet and a sink full of dirty dishes. So take care of *something*, anything: It can be a goldfish or it can be a plant. Whatever you choose to nurture, if you can make it flourish, you will too.

Acknowledgments

(Thank You Thank You)

THIS BOOK EXISTS because of the grace of two people: Brad Inman, who gave me the *Diary of a Flipper* column that later became *Diary of a Rookie* (available on Inman News, America's premier source of real estate news, *www.inman.com*), and Karen Murphy, acquisitions editor extraordinaire, who read my columns and thought, "Hey, that'd make a book."

Oh, make that three people: I could never have made it through this year without the constant support of Stephanie Losee, who would always take a pause from her own writing and her family to put up with my *agita* and build up my strength.

Thanks too to my terrific editors Jessica Swesey at Inman and Megan Gilbert at Kaplan, and to Trey Thoelcke for his wonderful copy edit and the rest of the Kaplan team: Josh, Michael, and Jennifer Farthing. My husband, Ivan Cohen, in addition to making dinner and bringing chocolates, greatly improved this book. Matthew Bank: love, and thanks for all the gossip about luxury floor plans. Plus, a shout-out to Matt Wagner of Fresh Books, my tireless superagent.

In some ways this book really started at the *New York Post*, and I'd like to thank the real estate team there, now led by Andy Wang, who I miss every single day. The success of the section was due to the hard work of Tamara Beckwith, Stephanie Bohane, Lacey Browne, Evelyn Cordon, Rex Dittman, Max Gross, Lisa Keys, and Peter Malbin, not to mention the late, lamented Michael Norcia. (No, I'm not forgetting Nathan, or the boys in The Bronx.) For freelancers, it sure seemed like Adam Bonislawski, Katherine Dykstra, Jason Sheftell, and Dakota Smith were around a lot, and I owe you all drinks. Braden Keil and Jane Reilly Mount were the easiest columnists in the world to work with.

I'd also like to thank Geoff Booth, John Crudele, Michelle D'Almeida, Ralph D'Onofrio, Robert George, Mary Huhn, Keith Kelly, Marcia Kranes, Vin Montuori, and Michael Shain of the *Post* for their various kindnesses.

Bignormous gratitude to all my clients, especially Persephone Miel for taking the leap of being first. I've also learned so much from Barbara Corcoran, Michael Daly, Ardell DellaLoggia, Mike Edelhart, Brenda Florida, Dottie Herman, Pam Liebman, Shaun Osher, Fred Peters, Diane Ramirez, Glenn Rice, Michael Shvo, Elizabeth Stribling, and Jacky Teplitzy. Ken Baris and Daren Hornig, thanks for the lunches. Props to Shaun Donovan for working mightily to keep this a great city for all New Yorkers. Dan Gerstein, thanks for all the wonderful and patient advice, and Gil Neary, thanks for being the absolutely perfect boss.

Hullo media friends: Lockhart Steele at Curbed.com; Joyce Cohen, Willie Neuman, and Claire Wilson at *The New York Times;* Stuart Elliot and Amir Korangy at *The Real Deal;* Bob Hagerty and Laura Lorber at *The Wall Street Journal;* Alan Heavens at the *Philadelphia Inquirer;* Sascha Brodsky at the *New York Resident;* Nicole Bode and Orla Healy at the *New York Daily News;* Sara Bonisteel at FoxNews.com; Shanti Marlar at *Us Weekly;* Trent Straube at *The New York Blade.* Thanks Chris Healy for putting me in *Glamour* and Barbara Wagner for dinner at Nobu 57. A wave to all my electronic buddies at WiredNewYork.com, and to Property Grunt. Kristen Shaughnessy at New York 1; who knew a TV star could be so phenomenally kind?

Thank you.

For being good friends who cross all categories: Moira Ariev, Amy Bruckman, Alan Cohen, Kevin DeGeeter, Alan Deutschman, Mark Fefer, Nancy Goldstein, Peter Hemmel, Janet Huege, Stephanie Jo Klein, Beth Lambert, Ron Lieber, Doug Mao, Dallas Middaugh, Jo Murray, Karen Petrone, Maria Romano, Karen Scanna, Jessica Sewell, Tom Unger, and John Wyatt. Kelly Kreth and Kaja Perina, the work you sent me kept me from starving to death. Ellen Macleay, I appreciate your being a fan before anybody else was. Todd Pruzan, formal thanks for providing a character reference for my husband.

Judge Judy, Howard, Debra, Greg, Steve, Joe: thanks for not throwing me out. Nancy, Joel, Harvey, Paula, Alan, Barry, Ann: thanks for inviting me in. Love to Jason, Julie, Colin, Shira, and Samantha. Jim and Nancy, there's no way to repay you—here's to many, many more adventures.

Thanks to Bruce Rubenstein and Michael Fleisher for rebuilding me, and to Peter Getty, Bill Oakley, Jon Handler, and David Gaffen for at various times suffering my nonsense. If the chapter on graciousness rings true at all, it's because of the warmth and hospitality of Rheta Bank, of blessed memory, and of Cynthia and Bernie Zucker.

If this book is persuasive, it's because I have had the greatest writing advisors anyone has ever had: Ann McCollum and Sally Laidlaw in high school; Mike Berthold, Mary Thomas, and the late Paul Marx at Harvard; Julie Connelly, Colin Leinster, and Bill Saporito at *Fortune;* and Faye Penn and Col Allan at the *Post*. Mark O'Donnell tried hard to teach me funny bits, and Kalia Doner, Elinor Nauen, and Steve Brill straight ones. If I've failed, well, my teachers did the best they could.

Finally, to my father Arthur: wherever my home is, the remembrance of your love and wisdom will be there too.